A Journal 1811

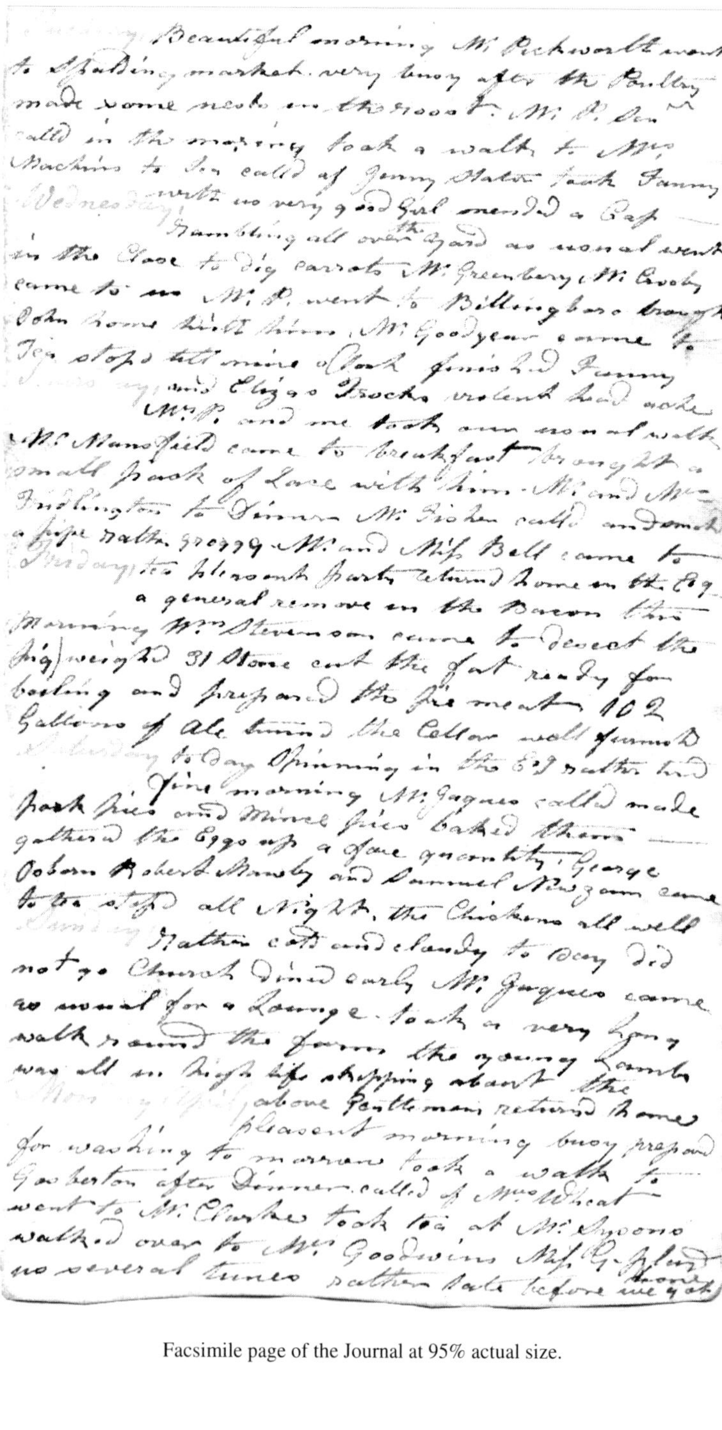

Facsimile page of the Journal at 95% actual size.

A Journal 1811

The Diary Of
A Lincolnshire
Farmer's Daughter

By Elizabeth Corney

Transcribed and Edited by
Audrey & Philip Walker

**Published by
Walker's Books Ltd.**

This Book Is Dedicated
With Love To
Our Grandchildren

Alice and George

Published by
Walker's Books Ltd. Oakham, Rutland. U.K. LE15 6AH.

ISBN 0955119707 (13 Digit 9780955119705)
First Published 2005

Printed and bound in Great Britain by
The Alden Press Oxford

Contents

Illustrations

The woodcut vignettes used throughout the Journal are from the late eighteenth and early nineteenth century works of Thomas Bewick.

Introduction

This Journal of 1811 was found in a bundle of old family documents and photographs handed down by a great uncle who lived in Belton-in-Rutland. The connection of the Journal with the village at that time was unknown.

It was a small, homemade notebook of laid paper covered in rough, faded Manilla and hand sewn at the head with white thread. The entries for each day, monthly accounts and songs were written in brown ink in a fine hand, but they were so small that a magnifying glass was required to decipher the text.

The author recorded neither her Christian name nor her surname but on April 6th 1811 she wrote, "This day marks the third year of our residence at Kirk Hill." It was the only clue to her identity but research established that in 1811, Kirk Hill Farm in the parish of Quadring, Lincolnshire, was leased from the Bishop of Lincoln by Jonathan Gleed of Donnington and his tenant was Andrew Corney.

Andrew Corney had married Mary Bardney at Folkingham in April 1784 and it was there that their two daughters were christened in the parish church, Mary in 1785 and Elizabeth in 1788. Elizabeth Corney has now been identified as the author of the Journal but at the time of her birth, the family were living in the hamlet of Laughton, a collection of three or four farmhouses about two miles south of Folkingham.

Almost certainly, this was the first of Elizabeth's Journals. From writing a very basic record at the beginning, she soon developed into an accomplished diarist. Aged 23 years, she recorded a year at Kirk Hill, an isolated farm house set deep in the flat landscape of the Fens, close to Gosberton but in the parish of Quadring. There was the constant stream of visitors, outings to the local fairs and statutes, pig killing, cheese making and the agony of toothache and the ague. She also noted more wide reaching events – the Great Comet of 1811, soldiers passing on their way to Norwich, correspondence from America and a visitor's return from China with souvenirs.

The Corney sisters were to marry two brothers of the Osborn family of Bourne. In 1814, Mary Corney married Thomas Osborn in Quadring church and thirteen years later in 1827, at the age of thirty-nine years, Elizabeth married his brother George, eight years her junior also in Quadring. Both of these future husbands were visitors to the Corney household and Thomas was referred to in the journal as "Cousin."

Thomas and Mary Osborn, Elizabeth's elder sister and brother-in-law continued to live at Kirk Hill Farm and Thomas was listed on the register of electors in 1832, qualifying for a vote by paying rent in excess of £50 per year.

Further research is needed to find where George and Elizabeth Osborn began their early married life but the link with the Journal being found in Belton-in-Rutland was discovered when the 1851 census of that parish revealed the couple living in Westbourne House, a fine Queen Anne residence. Living with them was George's unmarried sister Elizabeth Osborn (Cousin Betsy in the journal). George's occupation was given as "proprietor of houses" while later census returns recorded "retired farmer." Perhaps the name of this historic house dates from their time there.

In August 1862, Elizabeth Osborn died childless aged 73 years at Westbourne House, but it was to be another 23 years before George Osborn joined his wife. Their tombstones lie side by side to the west of the church porch at Belton-in-Rutland.

Audrey and Philip Walker

Acknowledgements:-

Lincolnshire Archives.
Spalding Gentleman's Society.
Lincolnshire Family History Society.
Mr David and Mrs Sally Spridgen of Kirk Hill Farm, Quadring.
Mrs Shelia Storer of Westbourne House, Belton-in-Rutland.
Mrs Julie Banham for the loan of the journal.
The late Archie Ringrose for preserving this document.
Most importantly, Elizabeth Corney who recorded her life as a farmer's daughter in the Fens in 1811.

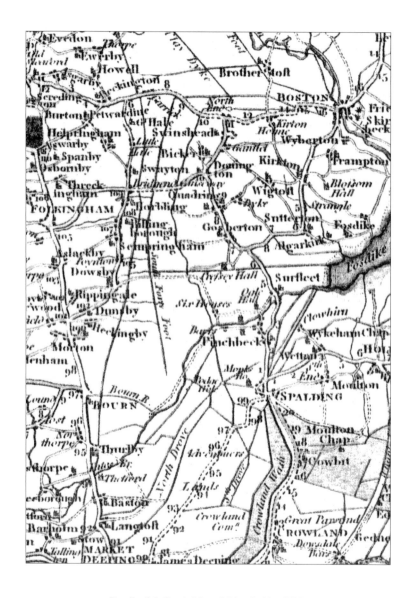

Detail of J. Cary's Map of Lincolnshire 1787.

JANUARY 1811

Tuesday 1st.
Mother unwell in the morning - wrote a letter to send to Bourn but was disappointed in sending it - bottled some old ale off - very cold day.

Wednesday 2nd.
Busy ironing and mangling all day - the weather very bad - frost and snow - played at cards in the evening.

Thursday 3rd.
Very busy all day - Nanny went to Mr. Brockelsby to have her finger dressed - made some caps up in the evening.

Friday 4th.
Nothing very particular happened today - the weather as usual - excessive cold and uncomfortable - pig weighed twenty-four stone all but two pounds.

Saturday 5th.
As usual a very throng[1] day - assisted in salting the pig and tunning[2] the beer - one hundred and four gallons - very high east wind - was obliged to make a fire in the parlour on account of smoke.

Sunday 6th.
Was not at church - the weather cold and frosty - John Rudkin brought the newspaper - stopped tea and supper.

Monday 7th.
Making pork pies - Mr. Wheat called and lunched with us - Mr. Osborn and Mr. Bellamy came to dinner - Mr. Bellamy was in pursuit of a farm very near us - received a letter.

Tuesday 8th.
Fine morning - Mr. Osborn and Mr. Bellamy returned home - sent a letter by them - baked some gingerbread in the afternoon - Mr. Johnson arrived in the evening as usual with a budget of news.

Wednesday 9th.
Snowy morning - Mr. and Mrs. Rudkin came to tea and spent the evening - Mr. Daybell came on some parish business.

---

[1] throng – busy.
[2] tunning – barrelling.

1

JANUARY 1811

Thursday 10th.
Cut a large quantity of patchwork out in the morning - prepared some small trifles for our journey - began to thaw in the evening - rained fast at eight o'clock.

Friday 11th.
The weather much the same as yesterday - nothing particular happened in the course of the day.

Saturday 12th.
Rainy morning - busy packing up clothes in the afternoon - played at cards in the evening - Mr Crane called for taxes.

Sunday 13th.
Was not at church - fine morning - Thomas Osborn came to dine - rain in the evening.

Monday 14th.
Rainy morn - set off to Bourn at 10 o'clock - arrived at 2 - very much fatigued - played at cards in the evening.

Tuesday 15th.
Bourn Sessions - Mr. Newzam and Mr. Mawby dined with us - walked up to the shops in the morning and was much amused – Mr. Johnston and a party to tea - stopped till 2 o'clock.

Wednesday 16th.
Sat down to work in the morning - Mr. Newzam returned home - went to Mr. J. Osborn's to tea and spent the evening - very pleasant.

Thursday 17th.
Took a long walk in the town - Miss Broughton and Miss Newzam came to dine - stopped all night - Miss Mawby came in the afternoon - our amusement in the evening was cards.

Friday 18th.
Large party of us took a walk in the town - the ladies returned home - took our tea and supper with Mrs. Osborn - went to sleep with my cousin Betsy - talked till 2 o'clock in the morning.

JANUARY 1811

Saturday 19th.

Fine morning - called of Miss Aland - played us several tunes - dined with my aunt - spent the evening with my cousin John - amusement was music, singing and cards - Betsy and I returned to rest at 12 o'clock.

Sunday 20th.

Went to church in the afternoon - took a walk with my cousin John down the new road - Miss Mawby returned home after 9 p.m. - Betsy and John Osborn stopped for supper.

Monday 21st.

Went to dine with John Osborn - called of Mr. J. Osborn, Mrs. Pare and J. Mawby - found him rather better - called at Mrs. Shipley's and Mr. Bailey's - received several invitations - played at cards in the evening.

Tuesday 22nd.

Took a long walk with Betsy Osborn after breakfast - Mr. John Gibson married this morning - came home to dine - Miss Lacey, Miss Andrews and Miss Smith to tea - spent the evening with amusements - singing and cards.

Wednesday 23rd.

Took a ride to Grimsthorpe Castle in a chaise - my cousin John went with us - saw a great deal in a little time - was highly delighted with the curiosities - went to Mr. Bailey's to tea - spent the evening very pleasantly.

Thursday 24th.

Went to Thurlby to dine at Mr. Mawby's - eight in number - we were conveyed in an open landau - played at cards in the evening - Betsy Osborn and myself withdrew ourselves at an early hour.

Friday 25th.

Fine morning - a large party of gents to dine with us - played at cards and forfeits - singing etc., etc. and altogether a very pleasant and agreeable evening.

Saturday 26th.
Miss Mawby returned home with us by the same conveyance as we went - dined with my aunt - went shopping in the afternoon - the same party met at Mr. Andrews to tea and spent the evening - went home at 11 o'clock.

Sunday 27th.
Cold morning - wrote a letter home - sent it by the boy - my cousin John, Elizabeth, Robert and Mr. Julds dined with us - took a walk in the fields after dinner - went to the evening lecture - received a note from Miss Smith respecting the same tomorrow evening.

Monday 28th.
Frosty morning - took a walk with Miss Osborn - Mr. Richardson called and lunched - sat chatting a long time - went up to Mr. Osborn's shop in the afternoon - purchased a few articles and drank tea - spent the evening at Mr. Smith's - large party - stopped till 1 o'clock - I unluckily got a fall but did not receive any hurt.

Tuesday 29th.
Charming fine morn - busy packing up our clothes - went to my cousin's to wait for Mr. Mawby - he arrived at 11 o'clock - we set off immediately - stopped a short time at Billingborough - dined at Donnington - called of Mrs. Gleed after dinner while the gents took their wine - we proceeded on our journey - got home to tea - was not in the least fatigued only rather cold - played at cards in the evening.

Wednesday 30th.
Sharp frosty morning - Mr. Osborn and Mr. Mawby returned home after breakfast - was rather uncomfortable - I did not feel inclined to do much work today - Mr. Jacques called to lunch with us.

Thursday 31st.
Very busy this morning - salting the pig and rendering the fat - a very unpleasant day - wind very high and snow for most part of the day - began to rain in the afternoon - played at cards in the evening.

Expenses for the month of January:-

	£	s	d
1 Pr. Pattens	0	2	3
Strings do.	0	0	3
Comb	0	1	6
Do.	0	0	6
Scissors	0	1	0
Rose Oil	0	2	0
Coloured paper	0	0	6
Servant	0	1	0
Laces	0	0	8
Handkerchief for present	0	2	2
Servant	0	1	0
Dinner	0	2	0
Servant at Lord Gwydir	0	1	0
	0	14	10

Morton's print of Quadring Church (1843).
It was here Elizabeth recorded, "Some of the congregation were asleep during the service. Mr Wilson in a loud and clear voice ordered the dog whipper to go round and keep them awake."

FEBRUARY 1811

Friday 1st.
February begins with cold and cloudy weather - was very throng all day making pork pies and mince pies, baking and churning - assisted in making the sausages after tea - played a game of cards after we had done.

Saturday 2nd.
Tolerable fine day for the season - cleaning rooms all the morning - sat down to patchwork in the afternoon - nothing very material occurred in the course of the day.

Sunday 3rd.
Did not go to church - Mr. Jacques called in the morning to inform us he had taken the farm for a friend - was very much disappointed to hear it - wrote some receipts[1] out in the evening and made out the bill of expenses for the last month.

Monday 4th.
Making preparations for washing - Mr. Wheat and Mr. Hall came in the morning - Mr. Willerton to tea - played a rubber[2] - stopped till 11 o'clock - wrote a letter to my cousin Ann which contained some curiosities.

Tuesday 5th.
Fine morning - busy washing all day - sent a letter to Miss Ann Osborn by Spalding - Mr. Jacques walked up after tea but did not stop long - began to spin a pound of flax yesterday.

Wednesday 6th.
Mr. Gleed came to course[3] in the morning - my Father was out - gone to Wigtoft - the rain water cistern was cleaned out - saw Mr. Cape in the afternoon - he was in wonderful great spirits - the wind was remarkably high in the night.

Thursday 7th.
Charming fine day - washed some small clothes in the morning - finished them by dinner - got them all dry and folded in the afternoon - mangling after tea - very little spinning done today.

---

[1] receipts – recipes.
[2] rubber – three successive games of whist or bridge.
[3] course – pursuit of hares with greyhounds.

FEBRUARY 1811

Friday 8th.
The wind remarkably high all day but did not rain - my amusement for the greater part of the day was spinning - wrote a note to Mr. Blackwell respecting the cistern - played at cribbage after supper.

Saturday 9th.
Delightful fine day - walked round the yard to take a view of the poultry then sat down to spin - Mr. Arnall Gleed called in the morning - my Father went to Donnington Market - Nanny went to town in the afternoon.

Sunday 10th.
Very dull unpleasant day which prevented me from going to church - was very much disappointed - Mr. Jacques came as usual in the morning for a lounge - wrote several sentences out in the afternoon.

Monday 11th.
Beautiful fine day - weaver brought a web of cloth home - twelve yards of hemp - Nanny went to see her Mother and stopped all night - my Father went to Donnington - spinning all day.

Tuesday 12th.
Several showers of rain fell today - my amusement was the same as yesterday - Nanny came home in the evening - received an invitation for tomorrow night - was not very well.

Wednesday 13th.
Received a letter this morning - met a very large party at Mr. Willerton's - in the evening we were summoned to the Assembly Room - danced two and twenty couples - first party sat down to sup at 11 o'clock - began to dance again and kept it up till 5 o'clock in the morning - tea and coffee was then introduced - went to bed at 7 o'clock - slept very little.

Thursday 14th.
Pleasant morning - walked in the gardens after breakfast - made several calls in the town - we walked in full procession from Mr. Doubleday's home - twelve in number – twenty-two sat down to dinner - played at blindman's buff and forfeits in the great room - signed them after tea - fine diversion - went to bed at 1 o'clock - very merry all evening.

Friday 15th.
Fine morning - took a walk - called of Miss Taylor - Mr. Beasley, Mr. W. and Mr. Dowse came to us - we walked round by the fields home - Miss Dowse went to Whapload – Mr. B. dressed in Miss Millington's pelisse and bonnet - walked through the town - very frightful he looked - played at cards in the evening.

Saturday 16th.
Cold morning - party decreased very much - gentlemen all went home at 3 o'clock this morning - we amused ourselves by reading and singing most part of the day - Miss Beasley went home in the afternoon - Mr. Willerton walked home with us after tea - called of Miss Millington but was not at home.

Sunday 17th.
Very ill all day - very bad cold and swelled face - could not go to church - felt rather low spirited - Mr. Jacques walked up in the afternoon but did not stop for tea - reading and writing was my amusement.

Monday 18th.
Frosty morning - cold very little better - made a petticoat in the morning - began to make a bonnet for Jenny Barratt's baby - cold a great deal worse this evening.

Tuesday 19th.
Cold day - my Father went to Spalding Market - ought to have sent a letter to Bourn but was rather unwell and could not sit down to write - finished making a bonnet - winding thread in the evening.

Wednesday 20th.
Weather still continues to be cold and unpleasant - took a walk to Jenny Barratt's - found the baby ill of the ague[1] and rather out of temper - called of Mrs. Rudkin as I came home - very busy spinning and winding thread again.

Thursday 21st.
Cold day - finished one length of the patchwork - two and a half yards long - Mr. Lumby called in the morning to settle a small account - Mr. Clarke and Mr. Butterfield, a Yorkshire man, came in the afternoon respecting the wool.

---

[1] ague – malarial fever, prevalent in the Fens.

FEBRUARY 1811

Friday 22nd
Rather pleasanter today than yesterday - finished winding and stringing the web - ten pounds to make two dozen napkins - began to spin the new flax in the evening - received a parcel from Boston.

Saturday 23rd.
No particular remarks on the weather today - cleaned all my shoes up and laid them by - walked down to the garden - Mr. John Laurence called to look at the beast - made a petticoat in the afternoon.

Sunday 24th.
Rainy morning - my Mother very ill - sent for Mr. Brockelsby in the afternoon - could not get to church today - Mr. Jacques came trembling and much alarmed at the sight of Fairbanks - writing in the evening.

Monday 25th.
My Mother still very ill - Mr. Brockelsby called in the morning - very busy washing - finished at 4 o'clock - made some custards in the morning - Mr. Clarke brought some rum - the weaver fetched the web - wrote a letter.

Tuesday 26th.
Pancake day - pleasant morning - my Father went to Mr. Newzam's with some beast for the fair - my Mother rather better - Mr. Brockelsby came in the evening - sent a letter to my cousin Ann - spinning part of the day.

Wednesday 27th.
Fine morning for the fair - my Father was late before he came home - Mr. Brockelsby called - my Mother very unwell - sent for more medicine in the afternoon - spinning some part of the day - heard that Mrs. Osborn was rather unwell.

Thursday 28th.
Stevenson came to kill the pig this morning - baking and churning - all confusion - my Mother rather better - Anthony Jackson called with a variety of curiosities - Mr. Emmitt's mistake - sent us four shillings short for eggs.

Expenses for the month of February:-

	£	s	d
Servant at Mr. W's	0	1	0
Patten strings	0	0	2
Cotton ball	0	0	0½
	0	1	2½
1 Pair shoes	0	6	6
	0	7	8½

Detail of Sang's print of Bourne circa 1860, with Osborn's shop to the left.

MARCH 1811

Friday 1st.
Fine morning - wonderful throng day - salting the pig, boiling the fat and cutting pie meat - one of the calves took in a doldrum - Mr. Brockelsby came in while we were at tea.

Saturday 2nd.
More work in hand today than yesterday if such a thing can be - made pork pies and mince pies - baked them - made some sausages - finished all by 9 o'clock - rather tired - played at cards in the evening.

Sunday 3rd.
Fine day but remarkably high wind - servants all went to church in the morning - cooked the dinner - walked to Gosberton church - an insignificant little dog thought proper to insult us - Mr. and Mrs. Rudkin and Mr. Jacques to supper.

Monday 4th.
Wind very high - settled over books in the small way for the year - Mr. Clark the little talkative tailor from Donnington called in the morning - sat a hen in the stable - spinning all day.

Tuesday 5th.
Fine morning but the wind rather high - my Father went to Spalding Market - walked to Miss Pickworth's after dinner - came home in the evening rather late - Mr. Rudkin arrived with a cargo of yeast - his first appearance since his arrival home.

Wednesday 6th.
Remarkable windy day - my Father went to Boston Market - Mr. Pickworth called at the gate in the morning - spinning all day, the old amusement - darned in the evening.

Thursday 7th.
Stormy day - went round the yard after dinner to gather the eggs up - found some difficulties in doing the same - Mr. Pattison called in the morning - my amusement the same as yesterday.

Friday 8th.
Rained very heavy all day - wind very high and unpleasant - spinning hard all day - one side of my face swelled as large as two and on that account could not accept Mrs. Pickworth's invitation for supper.

MARCH 1811.

Saturday 9th.
Pleasant morning after the rain - coloured two score handkerchiefs buff - finished spinning my pound of flax in the evening - lent my Father ten shillings and six pence to pay the labourers.

Sunday 10th.
Rather cold today - could not go to church - felt rather unwell in the afternoon - my Father went to Mr. Rudkin's after dinner - stopped till 9 p.m. - red cow calved.

Monday 11th.
Mild pleasant morning - finished making a bonnet - met with very good success in the egg trade today - hen began to hatch - brought three little chickens - in the afternoon toothache.

Tuesday 12th.
The weather very cold this morning - pulled and washed a quantity of wool - spread it in the garden to dry - paid due attention to the chickens - mending through the remainder of the day.

Wednesday 13th.
Fine day - the wind rather high - received a letter from my cousin Ann – dressed some fish for dinner - did not answer my expectations - went to Jenny Barratt's - called of Mrs. Rudkin - prepared for washing.

Thursday 14th.
Very large small clothes wash today - Jenny to help us - one of the chickens took in a very odd way - by proper care soon recovered - Mr. Newzam arrived at 5 o'clock - very much surprised us.

Friday 15th.
Packed up a hundred eggs and wrote a note - sent them to Mount Pleasant this morning - received a note from Mrs. Pickworth with thirteen duck eggs - charming day for drying clothes - Mr. Newzam returned home - mangling after tea - Mr. Jacques received a letter from Esq. Joaker what he had long expected - he came up immediately.

MARCH 1811.

Saturday 16th.
Delightful morning - the former part of this day is generally allowed for cleaning the house - sat a hen on thirteen duck eggs - wished her success - helped to iron - made an additional cushion for the gig to accommodate the driver of the same - 11 o'clock before I finished - quite fatigued and one finger bruised.

Sunday 17th.
Remarkable fine morning - I was left at home to keep house with dinner - the sun was very powerful so I treated the hen and chickens with an airing - went to Mrs. Rudkin's for tea and stopped for supper.

Monday 18th.
Rather cold today - starched and ironed some small clothes up - laid them by - gathered the eggs after dinner - took some bark[1] and wine - not very well.

Tuesday 19th.
Fine pleasant morning - Mr. Pickworth called - promised to go to dine with them on Sunday - Mr. Mansfield came after dinner to look at the wool - being a good parcel the business was soon settled - boiled eggs for supper.

Wednesday 20th.
This being the fast day walked to Quadring church in the morning - Miss P. and Miss Dixon sat with us - caught in a shower of rain coming home - rather fatigued - was beset again with a nasty little dog.

Thursday 21st.
Dull morning - made several new nests in the roost - they seem to answer very well - helped to churn and make the butter up - twenty three pounds - good market - Nanny went to the shop - rainy evening.

Friday 22nd.
Beautiful fine day - Mr. Mansfield came to weigh up the wool - assisted in getting the fleeces down - fine diversions - we had Mr. Jacques to help us - one hundred and forty one tods[2] to be delivered at Donnington Bridge - very good day's work.

---

[1] bark – possibly willow, an early form of aspirin.
[2] tods – a weight of wool, usually 28 pounds.

MARCH 1811.

Saturday 23rd.
Very fine day - served the lambs - very brisk and lively - sat a hen on thirteen duck eggs in the roost - gave the young chickens an airing - mended my stuff[1] gown - Mr. Johnson arrived in the afternoon - purchased a new morning gown - did not see Joe - was quite disappointed.

Sunday 24th.
Fine morning - wrote a letter to my cousin Ann - went to Mrs. Pickworth's to dine - being a clear day, we went up in the attic storey to take a view of the churches - very much amused us - took a long walk after tea to the new bridge - rather cold in the evening.

Monday 25th.
Sat down to work this morning making frocks for the children - Miss Thornton came to call upon Mrs. P. - stopped for dinner - very cheerful - walked part of the way home with my sister - called of Mrs. Smedley and Mrs. Cropley - Mrs. P. was rather fatigued - played a game of cribbage.

Tuesday 26th.
Beautiful morning - Mr. Pickworth went to Spalding Market - very busy after the poultry - made some nests in the roost - Mr. P. Senior called in the morning - took a walk to Mrs. Machin's to tea - called of Jenny Slater - took Fanny with us - very good girl - mended a cap.

Wednesday 27th.
Rambling all over the yard as usual - went in the close to dig carrots - Mr. Greenbury and Mr. Caveby came to us - Mr. P. went to Billingborough - brought John home with him - Mr. Goodyear came to tea - stopped till nine o'clock - finished Fanny's and Eliza's frocks - violent headache.

Thursday 28th.
Mrs. P. and me took our usual walk - Mr. Mansfield came to breakfast and brought a small pack of lace - Mr. and Mrs. Fridlington to dinner - Mr. Fisher called and smoked a pipe - rather groggy - Mr. and Mrs. Bell came to tea - pleasant party - returned home in the evening.

---

[1] stuff – warm, woollen fabric.

MARCH 1811.

Friday 29th.
A general remove in the bacon this morning - Mrs. Stevenson came to dissect the pig - weighed thirty one stone - cut the fat ready for boiling and prepared the pie meat - one hundred and two gallons of ale tunned - the cellar well furnished today - spinning in the evening - rather tired.

Saturday 30th.
Fine morning - Mr. Jacques called - made pork pies and mince pies - baked them - gathered the eggs up - a fair quantity - George Osborn, Robert Mawby and Samuel Newzam came to tea - stopped all night - the chickens all well.

Sunday 31st.
Rather cold and cloudy today - did not church - dined early - Mr. Jacques came as usual for a lounge - took a very long walk round the farm - the young lambs was all in high life skipping about the above - gentlemen returned home.

Expenses for the month of March:-

Bought of Mr. Johnson

	£	s	d
6¼ yds Print @ 22^d	0	11	5½
¾ yd Calico @ 12^d	0	0	9
	0	12	2½

On April 6th, Elizabeth recorded, "Today marks the third year of our residence at Kirk Hill." This is the only clue to her identity within the whole journal.

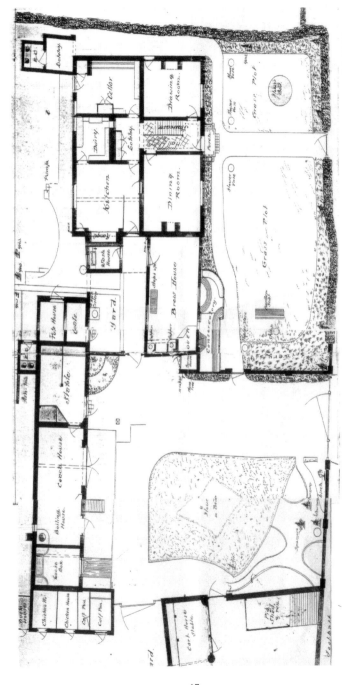

Kirk Hill Farm Quadring, from plans drawn for Thomas Osborn Esq. by Edward A. Jolly, Architect & Surveyor Dec. 9th 1890.
Reproduced by kind permission of Mr David & Mrs Sally Spridgen – the present owners.

17

APRIL 1811

Monday 1st.
Pleasant morning - busy preparing for washing tomorrow - took a walk to Gosberton after dinner - called of Mrs. Wheat - went to Mr. Clarke's - took tea at Mr. Syson's - walked over to Mrs. Goodwin's - Miss G. played us several tunes - rather late before we got home.

Tuesday 2nd.
Fine morning - busy washing all day - great wash and a few small clothes - got most of them dry - Mr. Gordon brought three beast home from Spalding Market - Fairbanks came to the door in a crazy fit - too tired to work in the evening - played cribbage.

Wednesday 3rd.
Charming morning - got all the clothes dry by dinner and part folded in the afternoon - Miss Clarke came to tea rather unexpectedly - walked great part of the way home with her - mangling in the evening.

Thursday 4th.
Fine morning - after the poultry as usual - carrying some clothes to the hedge, chanced to see Mr. and Mrs. Arnall surveying down the bank - coming to take a view of this new situation - ironing most part of the day - took a walk to Mr. Jacques's - carried them eleven dozen eggs.

Friday 5th.
The weather as usual - amusement for this day was spinning except some time that I spent in running after an obstinate and ill tempered duck - sent one hundred and forty four eggs to the shop - good market - came home - very bad cold - Mr. Jacques in tottering jest - stopped for supper.

Saturday 6th.
Beautiful morning - made the above duck lay in a proper nest that was made for her - sat a hen on eleven eggs in the henhouse - transplanted some geraniums - removed an hyacinth into the house - this day completes the third year of our residence at Kirk Hill.

Sunday 7th.
Cold day - went to Quadring church in the afternoon - Mr. Partridge preached - Mr. Joseph and Thomas Dodd and Richard Dodd and his brother Cadeb sat in our seat - Mr. and Mrs. Rudkin and Mr. John came in the evening.

APRIL 1811

Monday 8th.
Fine morning but very cold - my Father went to Folkingham Fair - came home to dinner - received a letter from my cousin Ann which announced their arrival Saturday week - a person with types and inks for marking linens came in the afternoon - purchased some letters with figures. Mr. Nall called.

Tuesday 9th.
The weather much the same - very cold - made some aprons - not much inclined for work today - black mare foaled - trade seems to go on very brisk in our line of business which at this time is very extensive - Mr. Jacques with a tale as usual - about the musicians.

Wednesday 10th.
Cold day - began to make our morning gowns - much the same as yesterday - very indifferent - wrote a letter - in the evening finished making one gown - had three shaking fits during the day.

Thursday 11th.
Very busy this morning - as usual after the poultry and eggs - sent ninety six to market - rolled twenty seven pounds of butter - good day's work - sent a letter with twenty two duck eggs to Bourn by Mrs. Bramley - hope they will arrive safe.

Friday 12th.
Good Friday - did not go to church - my Father went to Grantham after dinner - examined the duck eggs - was greatly astonished to find them all spretched[1] - very cold day - wind remarkably high - Mr. Rudkin in the evening - stopped for supper.

Saturday 13th.
Pleasant morning after the rain - helped to clean the best chambers - put the drawers to right - sat a hen upon duck eggs in the duck house and two hens upon thirteen eggs in the hen house - hen came off with twelve ducklings - all likely to do well - throng day indeed - violent headache.

Sunday 14th.
Very pleasant morning - did not go to church - was rather unwell - very dull day - never went out anywhere - writing in the afternoon.

---

[1] spretched – eggs that are cracked and on the point of hatching.

APRIL 1811

Monday 15th.
The weather as usual - had the duck house cleaned out - marched the goslings out - sixteen in number - put the drawers in our own room in order - Mr. Pyecroft Junior called - the parish officer came for assessment - violent headache - obliged to go bed.

Tuesday 16th.
Rather cold morning - very busy after the poultry as usual - found them all right - washed the walls in our rooms yellow - looked very well - finished it by tea - mended some things for the wash - quite tired - slept in the B. chamber.

Wednesday 17th.
Fine morning - washed some small clothes - starched and dried some muslins - sent for some cardboard and wire for a box - Mr. Jacques called in the afternoon - full of Esq. Joaken.

Thursday 18th.
Mr. Stevenson came to kill the pig - busy churning - finished mangling and ironing - fitted the window curtain up - white hen brought off eleven chickens - began to make a box in the evening.

Friday 19th.
Very busy all day - took a walk to the pasture with the cows - made some pork pies and some cheese cakes - baked them - Mrs. Rudkin called with Mrs. Nott and Miss Smith from Ancaster - finished the above box rather late.

Saturday 20th.
Pleasant morning - cleaning rooms and the cupboards in the keeping rooms - hen brought off eleven ducklings - Mrs. Pickworth made us a present of some eggs - my cousins Thomas, Betsy and Ann Osborn came to tea.

Sunday 21st.
Dull morning - brightened up towards noon - went to Quadring church in the afternoon - rode behind Mr. J. Osborn - rather fatigued with the ride - called of Mrs. Rudkin after tea - met with Mr. and Mrs. Brown.

APRIL 1811

Monday 22nd.
Pleasant morning - walked down to the garden - Nanny went to Kirton Statue – Mr. Pickworth called as he returned from Boston - expected a party to tea but did not come - Mr. Stott came in the afternoon - Mr. J. and Miss Osborn went home in the evening.

Tuesday 23rd.
Rather warm today - went round to feed the poultry - sat down to work - made a little serve me [1]- had the headache all day - took a hen and eleven chickens to the fen barn after dinner - Mr. Doubleday called for assessment.

Wednesday 24th.
Cold morning - mended some clothes - frilled a shirt collar - was not very well - Mr. Baxter called in the afternoon for some land tax - curious man - diverted us very much - Brisk mare foaled this morning.

Thursday 25th.
Weather very pleasant - busy amongst the fowls and ducks - six grown surprisingly - walked to the town after dinner - met with a disappointment there - came home to tea - Mr. Ranby came in the afternoon.

Friday 26th.
Fine morning - Beauty mare foaled - dressed some sheep's tails - sat the ducks and a hen upon duck eggs - Mr. Kirk came to dinner - took a ride to Mrs. Pickworth's in the afternoon - Miss A. Osborn with us - Mr. and Miss Bell.

Saturday 27th.
Very fine day for Spalding Fair - Mr. Hubbard dined with us - sat a hen on fifteen eggs - took a walk on the bank - called of Mrs. Thompson - Mrs. Smith Creasey called about a servant - Mr. Kirk called us up at about 11 o'clock - rather tipsy.

Sunday 28th.
Pleasant morning - John drove Ann and myself to Quadring church - heavy storm - thundered and lightened - rather alarmed us - Mrs. Seward lent us great coats - did not receive any wet - Mr. Kirk returned home - after tea took a walk down the Westhorpe.

---

[1] serve me – meaning unknown.

APRIL 1811

Monday 29th.
Showery day - dressed some sheep's tails for dinner - liked them very well - made a cap for myself - Nanny went to Mrs. Robinson's to be hired - Mr. Noble called to settle a small account - sat a hen in the coal house - thirteen eggs - hope to have a good increase.

Tuesday 30th.
Cloudy morning - my cousin Ann and Mary went to Mrs. Pickworth's - the fourth and last mare foaled in the night - had the dairy cleaned and whitewashed - dressed some more sheep's tails for dinner - finished making a cap - spinning in the afternoon - rain in the evening.

Expenses for the month of April:-

	£	s	d
½ yd Cambric muslin	0	1	0
Letters and ink for marking	0	1	3
Ferret[1] for morning gown	0	0	6
Cambric buttons	0	0	10½
1 Pair gloves	0	2	4
	0	5	11½

---

[1]ferret - a *stout cotton or silk tape.*

MAY 1811

Wednesday 1st..
Several showers fell in the course of the day - made the remainder of
these everlasting tails up in a pie - the fourth dinner made of them -
cellar and small beer place thoroughly cleaned - good day's work -
quite tired - Mr. Root came in the evening - found a nest of eggs.

Thursday 2nd.
Fine day - the poultry to feed and manage myself - very busy day -
baking and churning twenty seven pounds of butter - cleaned the
dresser drawers - Mr. Tomlingson called with cheese skins - a
traveller from Leicester with a variety of handkerchiefs - purchased
two Indian handkerchiefs from him.

Friday 3rd.
Pleasant morning - Mr. Stubbleday was married yesterday - brought
his lady home today - gay wedding I suppose - very busy cleaning and
scouring till late in the evening - Mr. Osborn came in about 8 o'clock
from Boston Fair unexpected.

Saturday 4th.
Up very early this morning - cleaned the sleeping rooms before
breakfast - general remove in the servants' room - whitewashed the
walls - finished by dinner - my cousin Ann and Mary came home in
the afternoon - the gents returned from Boston in the evening - Mr.
Pickworth called on his way home - was informed of a subject that
passed during the week respecting a gentleman not far off.

Sunday 5th.
Mr. Osborn returned home this morning - began to rain and was
prevented from going to church on that account - miserable day -
sheep came home from Boston Fair - Mr. Jacques walked up as usual -
was not very well.

Monday 6th.
Fine morning - washing all day but was very merry and much amused
by a subject that took place at the time we commenced washing - Mr.
Newzam dined with us on his return home from Boston Fair - Jenny
Barratt could not come to help me.

MAY 1811

Tuesday 7th.
Wet morning - Mary very unwell - sent for Mr. Brockelsby - washing all day - my cousin assisted me - Miss Millington was married this morning - went to church in a single horse chaise - Miss Dowse and Miss Simms attended as bridesmaids.

Wednesday 8th.
The weather rainy and unsettled - Ann and me went to Spalding Statute[1] but did not hire a servant - dined at the inn with a pleasant party - visited most of the principal shops in the town - the crowd being so large the streets were almost impassable.

Thursday 9th.
Rained the whole of the day - my Father went to Folkingham Statute - hired a boy - made a call at the barn as he came home - found a curious party there enjoying themselves - he very soon dispersed them and kicked up a pretty breeze among them.

Friday 10th.
Very busy all day - the brew house and kitchen thoroughly cleaned - ironing and mangling - laying clothes by - finished by tea - we felt ourselves completely jigged up - wrote a letter to my cousin Mary - sewed in the evening.

Saturday 11th.
The weather very fine - my Father went to Bourn Statute - hired a servant and one that we knew - busy cleaning the house - Mr. Naylor called for the Easter offering - hen brought of nine ducklings - lightened in the evening.

Sunday 12th.
A dreadful thunderstorm - a fire ball fell in the Risegate - was very much alarmed - Nanny could scarce keep me from fainting as we were left at home alone - Mr. Richard Dodd dined with us - letters and parcels arrived from Bourn - took a walk in the afternoon.

---

[1] Statute – a fair for the hiring of servants.

MAY 1811

Monday 13th.
The weather very hot - washed a few articles - dried and mangled them before dinner - Mr. Fiddles arrived in the Westhorpe - began to net a tippet[1] - took a walk in the evening - called upon Mrs. Rudkin - sheep came from Folkingham.

Tuesday 14th.
Very busy this morning - Nanny left us - several chickens fell in hysterical fits but soon recovered - assisted Ann in making a gown for my Mother - Mary Taylor called in the afternoon - Jenny Barratt to milk - the poor old drake gave up the ghost.

Wednesday 15th.
Pleasant morning - began to make our pink gowns - the front garden was cleaned and dressed over - Mr. Pickworth and gentlemen called as they came from Boston Market - singing in the evening as usual.

Thursday 16th.
The weather as yesterday - Ann and me sat down to work early this morning - two potter men came - purchased several pudding pots of them - helped to pull the geese in the afternoon - one gown finished - Robert Dowse came in the evening.

Friday 17th.
Very busily employed all the morning - baked bread - discovered a nest of eggs in the goose house - all the young poultry grown surprisingly - walked to Mr. Willerton's in the evening where we met two gentlemen merely to satisfy their curiosity - called at Mr. Syson's - Mrs. Syson ill.

Saturday 18th.
More work on this day than usual - upon the grand bustle till 4 o'clock - went round to gather the eggs accompanied by A. Osborn - a great rat beset us which alarmed us very much - a hen brought off fourteen chickens - my Father went to Donnington Market - rained in the evening.

Sunday 19th.
A miserable cold day - could not go to church - rained all day - the wind very high - without a servant - was amused in the evening by a party of weddingers on parade - Miss D. and her brothers with them.

---

[1] tippet – a short cape.

MAY 1811

Monday 20th.
Weather continues to be very cold and windy - hen brought off ten chickens - one pink gown finished - cottage bonnet in hand - our new maiden made her first appearance here - heard from Bourn.

Tuesday 21st.
Pleasant day - assisted my cousin Ann as usual in the business of dress making - took an early tea and walked to Gosberton - met with two gents at Mr. W.'s shop who frequently visit there - called upon Miss Simms but was not at home - disappointed.

Wednesday 22nd.
Cloudy morning - took the cows to the pasture - my employment the same as yesterday - duck and hen brought off sixteen ducklings - nothing more occurred worthy of attention during the day.

Thursday 23rd.
Pleasant morning - busy as usual on this day - churning and making up butter - baked bread - my cousin Ann and self walked down to the garden - gathered some gooseberries - made pies and custards.

Friday 24th.
Very showery day - assisted in dressing feathers for the middle room bed - quite completed it by noon - washed the ceiling and side walls once over - a woman with pots came - purchased a pair of dishes.

Saturday 25th.
The weather particularly warm - cleaning rooms as usual - saw several people pass going to Donnington - heard that Mrs. Pickworth was confined - received a cap from her - very pretty shape much admired it.

Sunday 26th.
Very sultry morning - my cousin Thomas came to breakfast - my Father, Mother and Ann went to Quadring church - very heavy storm of thunder and lightning at 1 o'clock - came on again towards the evening and continued the whole night - the lightning was dreadfully bad.

MAY 1811

Monday 27th.
My Father and Thomas went to Donnington Fair - very sultry and hot
- Mr. Shipley and Mr. O. for tea - they stopped till a late hour - my
Father bought a mare of Mr. S. - had a violent sore throat which
prevented me from sleeping the whole night.

Tuesday 28th.
Dull, cloudy morning - my throat very little better - Mr. Arnall Gleed
came with a builder to take an estimate of some building - he
prescribed a remedy for the above complaint which was of great
service - very cold in the evening - sat upstairs to work.

Wednesday 29th.
This was rather a busy day - brewing and ironing - rained all day - I
was obliged to keep a strict eye over the young poultry on account of
the wind being so tremendously high - Mr. J. Rudkin brought the
paper.

Thursday 30th.
Very hot day - Mr. Blackwell to repair the fireplaces - twenty five
pounds of butter churned - made the cheese - mangled some clothes -
walked to Gosberton after tea - called upon Miss Simms - had a
serious chat respecting a wedding a short time since.

Friday 31st.
Marked some stockings and had several little matters to arrange
during the day - one hundred and four gallons of ale tunned - three
gallons of currant wine bottled off - baked bread etc. etc. - finished
netting a tippet for Miss A. Osborn - heavy shower of rain in the
afternoon attended with thunder.

Expenses for the month of May:-

	£	s	d
May 3rd 1 Pair shoes	0	7	0
Bill at Mr. Everard's	0	10	6
Shoe strings	0	0	3
Paid out Mr. Dodd	0	5	6
5 yds Pink gingham	0	10	0
4½ yds Jean[1]	0	9	0
Brown Holland[2]	0	1	3
Buff print for aprons	0	1	9
Book muslin [3] - cotton wool	0	1	1
½ yd 3 nails[4] footing	0	2	4¾
1 yd Sarsenet[5] ribbon	0	0	8
1½ yd Narrow ribbon	0	0	3
¾ yd Scarlet ribbon	0	0	5¼
½ yd White	0	1	0
	2	11	1

---

[1] Jean – twilled cotton cloth.
[2] Brown Holland – unbleached linen fabric.
[3] Book muslin – muslin sold folded as a book.
[4] Nail - a measurement of cloth - 2¼ inches.
[5] Sarsenet – a very fine and soft silk fabric.

JUNE 1811

Saturday 1st.
Very pleasant morning - cleaned the sleeping rooms - prepared the dinner rather sooner than usual - my Father and Mother and my cousin Ann set off for Bourn in the afternoon - Mr. Cooper came to set up a bedstead.

Sunday 2nd.
Very dull miserable day - was not at church - Nanny thought of going but the rain prevented her - it came on very rapidly - lasted the whole afternoon - spent our day in reading and writing - my Father came home from Bourn at 10 o'clock in the evening.

Monday 3rd.
Pleasant morning - washed the middle room's walls over a second time - Mr. Johnson arrived at 2 o'clock - gave us an invitation to visit them at Stamford - purchased a bit of lace - made some ginger wine - began to net a tippet for myself - did very little of it.

Tuesday 4th.
Very dull morning - washed the walls blue for the last time - very well satisfied with the colour - sold thirty eggs in the evening - heard from Mrs. Pickworth - Mr. Jacques came up after tea - John began breaking the bay filly - Lady Gordon called.

Wednesday 5th.
Very pleasant morning - busy as usual - having all the poultry to shepherd and feed requires great attention - packed two hundred eggs for Mrs. Pickworth to send to London - a gang of very shabby looking men came in the evening about work.

Thursday 6th.
Showery morning - churned twenty pounds of butter - making cheese etc. etc. - the same disreputable party called again - one was rather troublesome - Mr. Dale favoured us with a short visit in the afternoon - he was very chatty - Miss Simms and her sister to tea - stopped all night - was much amused by different snippets they said.

Friday 7th.
Arose before five this morning - Miss Simms breakfasted with us and then walked home - finished netting my tippet - in the afternoon walked down to the garden - gathered some gooseberries - Mr. Arnall Gleed called in the evening at 7 o'clock.

JUNE 1811

Saturday 8th.
A remarkable hot morning - cleaning the rooms etc. - was very much fatigued by the heat of the weather - hung the hams up in the brewhouse - made some gooseberry pies and cheesecakes - my Father went to Donnington - thunderstorms very near us.

Sunday 9th.
Very pleasant morning - could not get to church - amused myself in reading and writing - had some peas for dinner first time - called upon Mrs. Rudkin after tea - met a large party in Mr. S's company.

Monday 10th.
Very busy this morning - baking bread etc. - cleaned all the rooms - my Father went to Bourn to dinner - began making a foundling cap for myself - my Mother came home in the evening - brought me a new gown.

Tuesday 11th.
Cool, pleasant morning - took a walk round the yard and garden to look at the calves and poultry - made a cap headpiece - packed up the sheet - measured the dimity[1] cover for the bed.

Wednesday 12th.
Fine morning - began making the bed - sat to work in the little room - three tailors came to make suits of clothes - very full house above and below - Mr. Willerton married yesterday - came home to dine.

Thursday 13th.
Working very hard at the bed all day - got the curtains up in the evening - Miss Pickworth and Mr. Fisher were married this morning before breakfast - very snug wedding - sheep washed today - butter and eggs advanced.

Friday 14th.
Pleasant cool morning - took a walk to Mrs. Pickworth's after dinner - found her in good spirits with a fine little girl - had the honour of drinking tea with the bride and groom and the bride's attendants – Mrs. Pickworth made us a present of some net and a piece of bride cake.

---

[1] dimity – cotton fabric woven with raised stripes.

JUNE 1811

Saturday 15th.
Rather warm this morning - busy cleaning the house - made some gooseberry pies and cakes - varnished the fireplace in the keeping room - Mr. and Mrs. J. Rudkin came to tea - stopped till 9 o'clock - gathered twenty four eggs - the chickens and ducks improve daily.

Sunday 16th.
Pleasant morning but rather warm - went to Gosberton church - quite fatigued with the walk - was favoured with a sight of the bride - made a very neat appearance indeed - white satin bonnet and tippet and lace veil - took a walk in the evening.

Monday 17th.
Very busy preparing for a large wash - baking bread - added a pint of brandy to the ginger wine and closed it up - mended some clothes for the wash - altered a cambric[1] tippet - worked till quite dark - wrote a note to Mr. Cooper - large party at Mr. W's.

Tuesday 18th.
Hot day - washing till 5 o'clock - got some of the clothes dry - Robert and George Osborn dined with us - received a letter from my cousin Ann - Nanny's sister came to dinner - the above gentlemen returned home after tea - sent some old straw for hats and bonnets.

Wednesday 19th.
The weather very pleasant - washing all day again - finished by tea - folded and mangled a large basket full in the evening - Mr. Cooper called for an order - sent a note and pattern of a cap to Mrs. Pickworth.

Thursday 20th.
Ironing and mangling all day from five in the morning till eight at night - when we completed the business everything was laid by - grass mowed in the front garden - coal house cleaned up - Mr. and Mrs. Morris arrived in the evening.

Friday 21st.
Cold stormy day - made a window curtain for the little room - finished making a buff apron - went down the garden to gather gooseberries - sent one hundred and twenty eggs to the shop and nineteen pounds of butter - mended some stockings in the evening.

---

[1] cambric – fine white linen.

Saturday 22nd.
Cleaning the house as usual this morning - baked some gooseberry pies - chine stuffed - couple of chickens pulled - a sheep dressed - wool house cleaned up - sent for a dozen white Barboni.[1]

Sunday 23rd.
Rainy morning - gathered some peas and prepared several other articles for dinner - Mr. J. Osborn, Mr. T. Osborn and Mr. Mawby with Sir Francis Burdett arrived at half past one o'clock - received some bride cake - the weather very unfavourable - could not walk today.

Monday 24th.
Wet morning prevented the clippers[2] from coming - Wingad came to pull the geese - overcasted some blankets for the white bed - had them washed - hemmed the valence for the window curtain - Mr. Pickworth sent the gig home.

Tuesday 25th.
Weather rather more favourable this morning - began to clip - making my jean petticoat - Mary-Ann Morris and Miss Roper called - took a ride to Gosberton after tea in the cartee - two men in liquor came to the door.

Wednesday 26th.
Pleasant morning - rained towards noon - was prevented from calling of Mrs. Morris in the evening - Mr. Wheat came in after tea - wet night.

Thursday 27th.
Fine morning - churned twenty eight pounds of butter - Mrs. Rudkin, Mrs. Morris and two young ladies came in - after tea went to Jenny Barratt's to take measure of children's heads for some bonnets - finished making an apron.

---

[1] Barboni – doves.
[2] clippers – sheep shearers.

Friday 28th.
Quarter before five as I was putting on my gown, was very much alarmed by a sudden flash of lightning followed by the most tremendous clap of thunder I ever heard in my life - Thompson, one of our labourers, had a fit on the occasion - made the bonnets and carried them home.

Saturday 29th.
Very cloudy morning - my Father went to Spalding Fair - Mr. Pickworth called to say he should not fetch Mrs. P. home - busy making furmety[1] for the clippers - Mr. Stevenson to make a mattress - assisted him in tacking it - walked to the town - the above party stopped till 1 o'clock - very good singing.

Sunday 30th.
Cool and pleasant this morning - Mr. Jacques came up - walked to Quadring church after dinner - took a long walk all round the farm after tea - did not walk less than nine miles - after supper rather fatigued.

Expenses for the month of June:-

	£	s	d
1 yd Lace	0	5	6
6½ yds Blue stripe	0	11	4½
¾ yd Shoe strings	0	0	3
1½ yds White Sarsenet ribbon	0	1	1½
25½ 3 nails muslin	0	6	6
¾ yd Narrow ribbon	0	0	3¾
Narrow satin ribbon	0	0	6¾
	1	5	7¼

---

[1] furmety – hulled wheat boiled in milk and sweetened with sugar.

JULY 1811

Monday 1st.

Cut the carpet out for the little room and made it - Mrs. Pickworth called as she returned from Spalding in a chaise[1] - brought a small parcel - repaired the servant's bed - Widow Hale brought the moping home.

Tuesday 2nd.

Fine morning - put four couple of ducks up to feed and six couple of chickens all to fatten - washed some small clothes - cleaned the best chamber ready for washing - altered a cambric petticoat in the evening.

Wednesday 3rd.

Ironing and drying clothes up - had the parlour cleaned - made a gooseberry pie - altered a cambric petticoat - helped to gather the currants for the wine - the cartee came home from the town - saved all the little jobs for the evening.

Thursday 4th.

Arose at half past four - rather a dull morning - made the wine - churned twice - my cousin Thomas drove us to Stow Green Fair - very pleasant day - Mr. J. Osborn and Mr. Mawby met us there - sixteen in number to tea - purchased some china and a pan.

Friday 5th.

Cleaning all day - painted the middle chamber and quite completed it - Marshall brought some goods from Stow Green Fair - very much annoyed by an impertinent little dog - bottled off some currant wine after tea.

Saturday 6th.

Cleaned all the china and silver - set them in the cupboard - Mr. Crane called for taxes - made some blackcurrant wine - brushed and rubbed the stairs down - going down the yard, met a hen with thirteen chickens coming up - from whence she came I know not.

Sunday 7th.

Cloudy morning - made some raspberry pies and assisted in preparing the dinner - my cousins Thomas and Mary arrived at one - my Father and Mother went to Quadring church - Mary-Ann Morris and Miss Roper came in the afternoon - wrote three notes in the evening.

---

[1] chaise – light, open carriage for one or two people.

JULY 1811

Monday 8th.
The front garden well cleaned - made a pound cake, cheese cakes and several other little articles - baked five times - gathered some raspberries for preserving - altered a white gown - went to bed completely tired.

Tuesday 9th.
Mr. Pickworth sent for the bull in the morning - invitation for us all to dine but could not go - severely disappointed - baked a gooseberry pie and some tartlets - keeping room, kitchen and brew house cleaned - ducks and chickens and geese pulled - Jenny Barratt to help on the occasion - the express arrived from Mount Pleasant but to no purpose.

Wednesday 10th.
Making tarts and custards and preparing the dinner - the ladies from Bourn arrived at one - Mr. and Mrs. Williamson and family from Aslackby - rained in the afternoon - danced after tea - very merry - walked down to see the grand race in the evening.

Thursday 11th.
A remarkable hot morning - Miss Everitt's pony ran away - Mr. W. and the ladies raced after it - I followed with a large wagon whip - Miss Williamson came to spend the afternoon with us - the musicians favoured us with another call - went to the race after tea - a party of ladies and gentlemen called in the night.

Friday 12th.
The weather very hot - music playing all the while we were at breakfast - danced a short time then took a walk down the Westhorpe - went to bed five in one bed after dinner - arose and dressed - went to Mrs. Rudkin's to tea - walked to the race after tea - a great deal of company stopped to supper.

Saturday 13th.
Expect a party to dine tomorrow - made some pastry - dressed some chickens - played at cards in the afternoon - Robert Osborn came to tea - was caught in the rain - sent 4 shillings worth of eggs to the shop - was disappointed of our walk in the evening.

Sunday 14th.
Very dull rainy morning - could not get to church - busy preparing
dinner - Mr. and Mrs. Pickworth, Mr. and Miss Thornton and Miss
Herring dined with us - a gentleman came in whilst at tea which
amused us very much - they returned home to supper - very merry all
evening.

Monday 15th.
Rather warm morning - Mrs. P. called as she passed by in search of a
servant - put the china and glasses by - shelled some peas for dinner -
walked to Mrs. Pickworth's to tea and very hot it was - caught in a
shower of rain coming home - quite fatigued.

Tuesday 16th.
The weather warm as usual - gathered some fruit for a pudding - made
some gooseberry pies - Master Shipley took tea with us - stopped all
night - walked to Gosberton in the evening - took some wine and cake
at Mrs. Syson's - called of Miss Simms - gone to Lincoln.

Wednesday 17th.
Awaked this morning at an early hour - very unwell - was not up to
breakfast - fruit pudding and a couple of ducks for dinner - my uncle
dined with us - gathered some fruit in the afternoon - Betsy Osborn
and Mary returned home after tea - felt very dull after they left us.

Thursday 18th.
Busy putting the house to rights - nothing very agreeable occurred
during the day - made a net skirt - mended some stockings - prepared
some clothes for washing - sat a hen on twelve eggs in the little stable.

Friday 19th.
Very dull morning but very close and hot - brewing all day - washed
some small clothes and mangled them - Ann and myself went in the
garden to get fruit - witnessed a terrible quarrel between a man and his
wife which lasted a long time.

Saturday 20th.
Cleaned the rooms - preserved some blackcurrants and raspberries -
made some redcurrant jelly - baked some gooseberry pies - dressed a
couple of chickens - sold two seats[1] of eggs to Mrs. Cumberworth -
mended gloves.

---

[1] seats – clutches.

JULY 1811

Sunday 21st.
A dull miserable day - could not get to church - rained the whole day
– my cousin Thomas came to dine - stopped all night - brought us a
parcel from John Mawby and a note from Betsy Osborn with a parcel
of combs - Mr. Jacques took tea with us.

Monday 22nd.
Rainy morning - Thomas and Ann went home after breakfast -
received a note from Mrs. Pickworth - Mr. Thornton came about 2
o'clock - drove us up to Billingborough to dine - met a large party -
danced till 2 o'clock in the morn - spent a very agreeable day - called
upon Mrs. Fisher and Mrs. Westmorland.

Tuesday 23rd.
Arose half after eight - took a walk with Miss F. Thornton to Mr.
Nelson's shop - my Father came for me - arrived home for dinner -
dressed and went to Mr. Brockelsby's to tea where we spent a very
pleasant evening - met a large party - danced thirteen couples - kept it
up till four in the morning - very much entertained - John drove me
home.

Wednesday 24th.
Rather fatigued this morning - did not breakfast till nearly eleven -
Mr. Thornton called as he returned from Boston - after dinner walked
to Mrs. Pickworth's - was obliged to sit down several times on the
road - brought some plants home - went to bed quite tired after three
days' fatigue.

Thursday 25th.
Did not feel quite well this morn - washed some table linen and sheets
up - finished them by tea - caught nine couple of fowls - put them in
the pen ready for Spalding Market - began making our blue gowns
after tea - Mr. Daybell called.

Friday 26th.
Pleasant morning - tied several jars of preserves down - Mr. Ward to
wind the wool - mangled some clothes and aired them up - Nanny
took the butter to the shop - sent three shillings worth of eggs - made
part of a gown - Mr. Brockelsby called late in the evening.

Saturday 27th.

Arose between three and four this morning - fed all the poultry - made the beds - helped to pile the wool - got it all in the low granary - cooked the dinner - excessive hot day - felt rather lazy - took a walk after tea in the hay field - spudded[1] a few thistles - brought the cows home.

Sunday 28th.

Particular hot day - Mr. Pickworth dined at Mr. Goodyear's - Mr. Newzam and Samuel came to dine with us - John drove us to Quadring church after dinner - a pious subject of the wool kind came to visit us in the church - took a long walk round the farm.

Monday 29th.

Pleasant morning - Mr. N. and Samuel went to Donnington after breakfast - came back to dinner - gathered some peas and beans and dressed a chicken for dinner - Mr. Osborn and George arrived at one o'clock - Mr. Dixon called to settle his account - wrote a letter to my cousins - after tea took a walk in the Risegate.

Tuesday 30th.

Cool and pleasant morning - packed eight couple of chickens and five couple of ducks - sent Nanny to Spalding Market with them - went to Caster's Bridge with her - Old Dolly trudged along with the luggage exceedingly well - very good market - came home - walked to the town after tea - saw Mrs. Willerton - very pleasant woman.

Wednesday 31st.

Removed the bacon from the rack - my Mother taken very unwell - obliged to go to bed after breakfast - Nanny helped to stack the hay - Joseph Pearson to prune the trees - made all the clothes ready for washing - Mrs. Rudkin came in the evening - made a frill for my pink gown.

---

[1] spudded – cut the roots with a sharp chisel hoe - a spudder.

Expenses for the month of July:-

	£	s	d
½ yd Lace footing	0	5	9
Sprigged muslin	0	1	6
2 yds White ribbon	0	1	8
Servant	0	1	0
Stiffened muslin	0	0	8
2 Combs 4^d	0	0	8
Parasol	1	1	0
3/8ths Linen	0	1	1½
Button moulds, round tape	0	0	3
	1	13	7½

Morton's print of Gosberton Church (1843).

Thursday 1st.
Arose this morning at half past four - washing the whole day from five in the morn till five in the evening – Mr. Wheat called for orders - after tea walked to the town - went to the Toll Bar for the sheep bill - called upon Mrs.Wheat and Miss N. respecting some work - called at Mr. Syson - Miss W. not very well - nine o'clock before we reached home - rather fatigued.

Friday 2nd.
Beautiful fine morning - very busy all day - ironing and mangling - got all the clothes aired up and laid by by eight o' clock - sent my bonnet to be altered - wrote to Miss Nicholson - began making a petticoat in the evening - rather tired.

Saturday 3rd.
Cool pleasant morning - cleaned our own rooms - made a wise[1] cheese - gathered some potatoes, carrots, cabbages and onions for dinner - made them ready for the pot - sat down to work in the afternoon upstairs - at 8 o'clock poured with rain.

Sunday 4th.
Pleasant day - my Mother and Father went to Quadring church in the morning - we walked to Gosberton in the afternoon - saw the account of the death of the fasting woman who lived four years without eating - Ann Moore of Tutbury in Staffordshire.

Monday 5th.
Preparing all our clothes for the great wash - had some celery and plants set in the garden - sent for a washer woman in the Risegate but was disappointed - she had gone to Gedney - Winger came to pull the geese - began to make a cap in the evening.

Tuesday 6th.
Busy this morning in the dairy and serving the poultry which is nearly all my employment before breakfast - began to wash some small clothes - got the vegetables and cooked dinner - Mr. Wheat called - Mr. Harrison brought me a letter from Spalding - about eight o'clock the wind arose alarmingly high.

---

[1] wise – meaning unknown, possibly sage.

AUGUST 1811

Wednesday 7th.
Up before five this morning - boiled some potatoes to send in the field - this day completes the hay harvest - washing all day again - got most of the clothes dry and folded - after tea walked to the town - felt quite fatigued with my day's work - Mrs. Willerton presented us with some very nice apples.

Thursday 8th.
Rainy morning - sat down to work while dinner - mangled a large basket of clothes - in the afternoon a very heavy shower of rain attended with loud claps of thunder - Mr. Arnall Gleed and little Joseph came to tea - had the misfortune to lose the old light duck.

Friday 9th.
Dull cloudy morning - making up clothes from the wash - finished a foundling cap - began harvest in the afternoon - had five chaldron[1] of coal in - was obliged to remove the white hen and family from the coalhouse - chickens grow hourly.

Saturday 10th.
Cleaned our own rooms before breakfast - fed the poultry as usual - gathered some plumbs - made a pie - prepared the dinner - Mrs. Rudkin sent for us for tea - did not go - Miss Weatherhog and Miss Digby came to tea - a very little girl went and sat round the kitchen fire.

Sunday 11th.
Particular cold morning - went to Aslackby Feast - dined at Mr. Newzam's - J. Osborn drove Miss Andrews and Miss Lacey over to B. Copes - my uncle and cousins came to dinner - went to church in the afternoon - took a walk to Mrs. Williamson's in the evening and Mrs. Broughton's - the parson supped with us - Mr. Osborn slept here.

Monday 12th.
Walked out after breakfast - called upon Mrs. Barwis and Miss Williamson - my cousins Thomas and Betsy arrived at twelve - dined at Mr. Williamson's - Miss and the two Mr. Goodsons there – Mr. Raddish played during the tea - we began to dance at seven o'clock and kept it up with great spirit till four the next morning when we all retired to rest a few hours.

---

[1] chaldron – measure for coal, 36 bushels or 288 gallons.

Tuesday 13th.

Pleasant morning - not the least bit fatigued after dancing - thirteen of us sat down to breakfast at Mr. W's - not a little noise - took a walk to the spring - we all partook of the waters which quite revived us - dined at Mr. Newzam's - Mr. Hall and family there - the same party all assembled at Mr. N's to tea where we danced the whole night - I never spent two pleasanter evenings in my life - walked up to Mrs. W's to sleep.

Wednesday 14th.

Mr. Newzam was in very great spirits - sang several songs and did everything but dance - the company begins to decline this morning - dined at Mrs.W's with Mrs. Fridlington - all went to the temple for tea - rode home in the evening - saw Miss Casswell fall from her horse - not hurt - passed Miss Goodson and John on the road to Millthorpe.

Thursday 15th.

Felt more unsettled and more fatigued than I had done all the feast - rather a key too low - could not be in spirits the whole day - brewing - putting all our clothes to right - did not dress till the evening - helped to carry the ale in the cellar after tea.

Friday 16th.

Fine morning - churning and cheese making - after dinner we locked up the doors and walked all round the farm - went to see them sheave - gleaned some wheat for the chickens - found four eggs at the barn - seven o'clock when we was home - Mrs. P. sent some yeast - returned the flower pots.

Saturday 17th.

Very busy all day - dressed a couple of chickens - got the vegetables for dinner - gathered all the plumbs and greengages - made three pies - bottled off some wine - one hundred and four gallons of ale tunned - helped carry some of the rubbish out the garden - mended me gloves - John Rudkin came after tea.

Sunday 18th.

Very warm morning - my Father and Mother went to Quadring Church - busy preparing for dinner - Thomas Osborn and John Mawby arrived at one - after dinner we took a ride to Fosdyke Inn where we met a numerous party - walked on the bank - spent a pleasant evening and returned home at ten o'clock - the above gents went home after supper.

AUGUST 1811

Monday 19th.
Cold and cloudy all day - gathered some French beans for pickling - made the cheese and prepared the dinner - made part of a gown what little time I sat to work - nothing more particular - only a very heavy shower in the evening.

Tuesday 20th.
Wet morning - had grass mown in the front garden - made some plumb pies - baked bread - had three hens with their families placed in the duck house - preserved some greengage plumbs - sat another hen in the roost - finished my blue gown - mended some stockings.

Wednesday 21st.
Dry morning for the harvest - altered my morning gowns and washed them - began to bleach a web of hemp - the chickens were very troublesome and required much attendance - man to catch the rats - bricklayers came to make the mortar up - three men began to cut the oats.

Thursday 22nd.
Pleasant day - after dinner walked to Gosberton - called upon Mrs. Syson - received a small present from Miss Weatherhog - invitation to dine on Sunday - saw several curiosities that John Willerton brought home from China - came home to tea - got very wet - my Mother had the ague in the evening.

Friday 23rd.
Fine morning - busy feeding the poultry as usual - churning and cheese making - rolled eighteen pounds of butter after dinner - sent it to the shop with one hundred goose quills - took a walk to Mrs. Rudkin's in the evening - was informed yesterday that Miss Hill and Mr. East were married last Wednesday.

Saturday 24th.
Remarkable hot morning - cleaned our own room - had very bad luck with some chickens - was obliged to mix up some fresh food for them - pickled some kidney beans - finished making some nightgowns - had a very violent cold and headache.

Sunday 25th.

Walked to Gosberton Church this morning - was caught in the rain - got very wet before we could reach the church - Mr. R. Cawthorpe offered us an umbrella - dined at Mrs. Syson's - met with Mr. N. Hilton - stopped all day - John drove us home to supper - Mr. Syson was away from home - fine evening.

Monday 26th.

Charming fine morning - sat down to work by nine o'clock - put five eggs under the hen in the roost that came from the Fen barn - the onions gathered up and brought into the granary - after supper sat down to write - wrote several songs out.

Tuesday 27th.

Fine morning - the wind very high - began to cart wheat - Nanny went to help them on the mower - carried the dinner to the barn - got rather wet in coming home - Mr. Stredder from Folkingham called as we sat at breakfast - my Father went to town - Mr. Syson sent us half a dozen pigeons.

Wednesday 28th.

Cold morning - my Father went to Spalding Fair - sold the little favourite nag mare to a gentleman of Wisbech that keeps a livery stable - dressed some pigeons - Bet Ward sent half a peck of damsons - finished making the nightgowns - gathered sixteen fine eggs.

Thursday 29th.

Sat down to work before eight this morning - finished making two shirts - rained very heavy - had all the chickens to get up - opened the large pin-cushion and drawed from there no less than twenty six needles - Mr. Jacques to tea - the rain prevented me from taking a walk.

Friday 30th.

Very pleasant morning after the rain - sat down to work very seriously till dinner was ready - took a long walk in the afternoon - called at the barn - brought home a hen and eleven young chickens - made two bottles of strong liquid for the hair - wrote some songs out.

AUGUST 1811

Saturday 31st.
Fine morning - gathered some sage for the cheese - breakfasted one hundred and nine young fowl - cleaned the sleeping rooms - cooked the dinner - my Mother carried it to the field - mended a pair of stockings - well satisfied with me day's work.

Expenses for the month of August:-

	£	s	d
2 Pair stockings 4/-	0	8	0
1 Comb	0	0	8
Shoe strings	0	0	3½
1 Pair gloves	0	2	2
3½ yds Ribbon for bonnet	0	1	11
Sarsenet ribbon for cloaks	0	0	6
Cotton lace	0	0	8
Servant	0	1	0
Jenny Barratt - altering	0	3	6
Edging & lining	0	2	0
Straw additional	0	1	0
	1	2	8½

Westbourne House, Belton-in-Rutland, marital home of Elizabeth and George Osborn.

SEPTEMBER 1811

Sunday 1st.
Cloudy morning - rode to Quadring Church - some part of the harness broke - was fearful we should be bundled out - some of the congregation were asleep during the service - Mr. Wilson in a loud and clear voice ordered the dog whipper to go round and keep them awake.

Monday 2nd.
Busy this morning laying clothes - by a bad misfortune happened the wagons ran over a couple of the finest ducks and killed them on the spot - preserved some damsons - added some more vinegar to the pickle - worked hard till nearly eleven o'clock in the evening.

Tuesday 3rd.
Washed some small clothes - Nanny helped to stack the barley - two very great strangers called upon us - Mr. East and his Father - the former is a school master and was going into Yorkshire in pursuit of a situation - Mr. and Mrs. Jacques took tea with us - a great fire alarmed us which appeared a long way off.

Wednesday 4th.
Four bricklayers came from Donnington this morning - began pulling the building down - seasoned the ducks for dinner - my Father went to Donnington Fair - came home and went to Bridge End to dine with Mr. Ward - Mr. Gleed came over in the afternoon - ironed up the clothes and laid them by.

Thursday 5th.
Three carpenters joined the above company this morning - the two masters, Mr. Barnet and Mr. Ellis dine with us every day - Mr. B. sports his pipe after dinner - washed twenty-two pairs of cotton stockings - took a walk to Mrs. Rudkin's - Mrs. R. gave us some bunches of lavender.

Friday 6th.
Sat very close to work this morning - making up new cloth - beautiful fine day - finished carting barley - a regiment of soldiers passed through Gosberton this morning with eight baggage wagons - going to Norwich[1] - gathered some nuts after dinner - over fatigued with laughing.

---

[1] Norwich experienced Luddite riots in 1811.

SEPTEMBER 1811

Saturday 7th.
A most delightful day for the harvest - immoderately busy as usual - cleaning a little - the men began taking the roof off - the yard was all dust and confusion - Mr. Gleed came and stopped all the morning - papered the table drawers in the blue room - twenty six eggs from the Fen.

Sunday 8th.
Great mist this morning but particularly warm after it cleared up - did not go to church - the day appeared rather long - Mr. and Mrs. Rudkin, Mr. John and Miss Roper to tea - no newspaper this week - a comet[1] has appeared in the sky these last three nights.

Monday 9th.
The morning very wet as yesterday - Mr. Richard Gleed and Mr. Arnall came to shoot – Mr. James Sidney spent the afternoon with us so we had no want of news today which made amends for yesterday - the building advances moderately.

Tuesday 10th.
A thick fog - very uncomfortable morning particularly for the young chickens - the sun had great power towards noon - finished making up the new cloth work - began to alter a muslin frock - finished carting the white corn - my Father taken very ill - was up most part of the night.

Wednesday 11th.
Very hot and dry - the comet still appears every night - a great scarcity of water - my Mother and Nanny very busy cleaning the front garden - Mr. A. Gleed came over in the morning - all the bricklayers and carpenters here today.

Thursday 12th.
Cool, pleasant morning - sat down to work early - finished the frocks - mended my lilac gown - made some tea cakes - Mr. Arnall Gleed is a constant visitor at Kirk Hill most days - the garden was quite completed - took a walk to Jenny Barratt's after tea.

---

[1] The Great Comet of 1811 was at its brightest during September and October. Visible with the naked eye for 9 months, it is the longest period of visibility of a comet on record.

Friday 13th.
Washed up a piece of cloth and some new sheets - Mr. Gleed Senior took a ride over in the chaise this morning - looks very ill and a great deal altered - eleven to dinner - cleaned the parlour - the harvest cart came home - three cheers was given at the sight of the brown jug.

Saturday 14th. (Sunday)
Pleasant morning - took a ride to Quadring Church - was almost choked with dust - disappointed of a visit in the afternoon - Mr. and Mrs. Pickworth called as they returned home from Mr. Fridlington's - John Rudkin came in the evening.

Sunday 15th. (Saturday)
Extremely sorry I should make such a grand mistake but hope the reader will excuse the error - it was merely for want of a better light - Saturday very busy all day - Mr. Brummer and Mr. Nicholls of Spalding called in the afternoon - Mrs. R. came.

Monday 16th.
Began to wash early this morning - finished by three o'clock - dressed and went to take tea at Mr.Wheat's - met with the Misses Mittens and Miss Simms - we left the town at eight - very unpleasant walk - the fog came on so quick we could scarce see the road though the comet appeared very brilliant.

Tuesday 17th.
Pleasant morning - busy preparing for Spalding Market - sent Nanny and Andrew with a cart load of ducks, fowls, eggs etc. - mangled the clothes - upon the full chase all day as usual - Nanny Liley called - brought a variety of flower seeds from Mr. Edmund's garden - tolerable good market.

Wednesday 18th.
Great day's work done today - brewing till late at night - received a letter from Bourn which announced my aunt and uncle's arrival on Sunday - made some ratafia[1] and queen cakes - happened very lucky in baking them - Mr. Gleed as usual - mended some stockings.

---

[1] ratafia – biscuits flavoured with almonds.

SEPTEMBER 1811

Thursday 19th.
Cleaned the chamber ready for washing - cooked dinner - Mr. Jacques came in - had a glass of wine and water - looked very ill - washed our own room and men's room - remarkable hot day - churned in the evening - quite tired with my day's work.

Friday 20th.
I think the weather still hotter today - made some cheese cakes, apple pies and tart crusts - Mrs. Pickworth sent us some pigeons - Mr. John Casswell, Wigtoft called with cousin - "How d'ye do?" - drank a glass and went off - I must say I was glad to see how the coat fitted.

Saturday 21st.
Very busy all day cleaning the house up - dressed some pigeons - it was after tea before I had time to change my gown - rained, thundered and lightened in the evening - played a game of cards.

Sunday 22nd.
Pleasant morning - busy preparing dinner - my aunt and uncle, Catherine and Miss Bellamy came about twelve - Mr. and Mrs. Wheat to tea - Mr. and Mrs. Rudkin to supper - sent two parcels by Mr.O. in the evening.

Monday 23rd.
Dull morning - rained great part of the day - sat at work all the morning - after dinner walked with my aunt and the children down to Mr. Jacques - returned home to tea - played at cards in the evening.

Tuesday 24th.
Delightful morning - did very little work today - my Father went to dine at Mr. Casswell's, Wigtoft - the Boston journey was concluded this morning during breakfast - walked to the town - took tea with Mr. Willerton - ordered the chaise at Mr. Brand's.

Wednesday 25th.
Terrible rainy morning - my Father went to Spalding Fair - sent a note to Bourn - had a fire in the keeping room first time - Mrs. Pickworth called in the afternoon going to the Fair - raised two card tables in the evening.

Thursday 26th.
Pleasant morning - sat down to work by nine o'clock - went to Mr. Rudkin's to tea and supper - stopped till eleven o'clock - highly entertained with his ramble in London - rather an unpleasant walk home.

Friday 27th.
Rained very heavy till noon - had a goose and a couple of fowls dressed - baked bread - cleaned all the chambers - seven of us took a ride in the sociable[1] to Mrs. Pickworth's accompanied by Mr. Cape - Mr. J. Osborn came - a very pleasant afternoon and evening - near two when we got home.

Saturday 28th.
Beautiful fine morning for our journey, but was disappointed of a conveyance by Brand - letting his chaise to another, we were under the disagreeable necessity of riding in a cart - was very much gratified with Boston, particularly the church - the weather proved rather unfavourable for us.

Sunday 29th.
Fine morning - did not go to church - was over fatigued with our journey yesterday - took a long walk in the fields after dinner - called upon Mrs. Rudkin - in the evening Mr. J. Rudkin supped with us - my aunt very unwell all night - rested very little.

Monday 30th.
The bricklayers made their appearance this morning after a very long absence - made a giblet pie - twelve sat down to dinner - today was fixed for my aunt going home but was prevented by the weather - Mr. Jacques spent the day with us - three card tables set out - I for a wonder was very fortunate.

Expenses for the month of September:-

	£	s	d
5 oz Lambswool 6^{d}	0	2	6
	0	2	6

---

[1] sociable – open carriage with facing side seats.

Tuesday 1st.
Weather very showery again this morning - my aunt and cousins left us about half past eight - family very much reduced - only three to dine - cleaned all the chambers and put the cupboards to right - thundered and lightened in the evening.

Wednesday 2nd.
Particular fine morning for the season - prepared the dinner - began to net my tippett but finding the net too small, was obliged to undo the whole piece - mended two pairs of stockings in the evening.

Thursday 3rd.
After the usual work of the morning, sat down to work till nearly eleven - made a sheep's tail pie for dinner which proved to be a good one - baked bread and cakes for tea - wet evening.

Friday 4th.
Five carpenters and two bricklayers came this morning - they raised the roof of the granary with several huzza's - the jolly brown jug was a welcome visitor amongst them - wrote a note to Mrs. Scarborough - the comet still appears.

Saturday 5th.
Cleaned the house all over - made an apple pie - Mr. and Mrs. Rudkin set off for Branston Feast early this morning accompanied by Miss Ann Smalley - played a game of cards in the evening.

Sunday 6th.
Very pleasant morning but did not go to church - Mr. Thomas Osborn brought home the gig[1] and a box of apples - Mrs. Sanderson came past in a chaise - received a parcel from Boston - wrote a letter to my cousin Ann.

Monday 7th.
Began this morning to prepare for washing - walked to Gosberton after dinner - met the Norwich shoemaker - engaged to meet him at the double roofed house but had no shoes to fit - ordered one pair of him - the large bush cut down in the paddock.

---

[1] gig – light, two-wheeled, one horse carriage.

OCTOBER 1811

Tuesday 8th.

Beautiful morning - began to wash nine weeks' clothes - washing all day continually - got a few of them dry - the little favourite cade[1] chicken got completely tipsy with drinking ale with the washers - sat down to a little work in the evening.

Wednesday 9th.

Remarkably fine for the season - washing all day again - Mr. Gleed came to course - one of the greyhounds which he valued at twenty guineas secured a terrible wound in her shoulder - obliged to shut it up - Mr. Gleed came again in the evening to visit the patient.

Thursday 10th.

Got all our clothes dry - ironing, mangling and laying by the whole day - my Father went to Swaton Fair early this morning - Mr. Gleed came for the dog - it walked home very well - Mr. Barnet began tiling the granary - preserved some white bullens[2].

Friday 11th.

Weather begins to alter very much - Mr. Gleed came again this morning - starched some fine linen and washed up the lace - finished all by three o'clock - we had just got dressed when Mr. Newzam and Miss Broughton made their appearance in the yard - played at cards in the evening.

Saturday 12th.

Pleasant morning - got up early to clean the keeping room - made an apple pie - Mr. Musson came to look at the shearlings[3] - Mr. Newzam took a ride to Donnington - my Father went to Folkingham after dinner - Mrs. Sanderson returned home from Mr. Pickworth's - played at cards in the evening.

Sunday 13th.

Cold morning - particularly high wind - was not at church - baked an apple pie and prepared the dinner - went out to assist them getting in the gig - the wind took hold of my bonnet and blew it a considerable way before I could stop it - Mr. N. and Miss Broughton returned home.

---

[1] cade – reared by hand.

[2] bullens – wild plums.

[3] shearlings – sheep that have been shorn once.

OCTOBER 1811

Monday 14th.

Rained most part of the day - began netting my lambswool tippet - finished it in the evening quite to my satisfaction - one of the wheels was fitted out for the first time this season but was not in time for going after such a long rest - sat up rather late to finish a little work.

Tuesday 15th.

Mild pleasant morning and continued so the whole day - took my white coat all to bits and began to make it into a gown - quite finished the skirt - Mr. Goodyear paid for the lamb - Mrs. Rudkin had an indifferent market for her geese.

Wednesday 16th.

Finished making the above gown - fits very well - the sheep went forward for Folkingham Fair - a very fine day for their journey - received an invitation to dine at Mr. Gleed's tomorrow but could not accept it - caught four mice in the new trap.

Thursday 17th.

Great number of people passing this morning - three and four on a horse - they appear very anxious to reach the gay fair at Donnington which I suppose is rather larger than usual on account of the weather being so fine - the fair at Folkingham was very indifferent - one expected a letter but was disappointed.

Friday 18th.

Fine pleasant morning for the season - finished making the close white gown - drew the pattern of the work out to send for some more from Mr. Willerton's - began to work a cap headpiece - Mr. Robert Smith called for some assessment - sat up till a late hour - rained fast.

Saturday 19th.

Very hot morning - found a hen sitting in Breach Lane on nine eggs - after the business of the morning over sat down to my cap working - my Father went to Donnington - took tea at Mr. Gleed's and ate some of Mr.Yerburgh's bride cake. - brought me pair of shoes home.

Sunday 20th.

Dull cold morning - Mr. Jacques walked up as usual - my Father went to Bourn to dinner - was not at church - was prevented from taking a walk - hen came off with seven chickens - received an invitation to dine tomorrow.

OCTOBER 1811

Monday 21st.
Rather cloudy this morning - went to Mr. Syson's to dine - spent a very pleasant day - met with Miss Maddison and Miss Hardy - walked to Mr. Cope's to hear the organ - highly entertained - after tea Mr. and Mrs. Syson favoured us with a duet.

Tuesday 22nd.
Tolerable good fair at Swinstead yesterday for the sheep - washed some small clothes up - determined upon saving the chickens' cakes as the one we had at hand before is likely to behave extremely well to them - Mr. Casswell came tearing like a lion choked with passion.

Wednesday 23rd.
Fine morning for our clothes' drying - rinsing, starching, ironing and mangling - finished laying them all up by tea - made a beginning to sow wheat - sat down to working a cap - finished the head hem and the little corner bit - played a game of cribbage.

Thursday 24th.
Particular fine morning - quite finished my cap and made it up - put on my old stuff gown for the first time this season - the chickens grow very fast - my Mother began to spin.

Friday 25th.
Marked off several different articles - cleaned six pairs of shoes and boots - the carpenters came to lay the granary floor down - Mr. Emmitt according to custom made a mistake in the shop bill.

Saturday 26th.
Rainy morning - cleaned our own rooms - put all my clothes in order ready for a journey - Mrs. Gordon brought no rise - Mr. Stubley came in very tipsy - played at cards in the evening.

Sunday 27th.
Went to Quadring Church in the morning just in time to hear the text - called upon Mrs. Seward - found her and the little babe as well as could be expected - had a very cold ride - Mr. Jacques to tea - beautiful night.

OCTOBER 1811

Monday 28th.
Beautiful pleasant morning - busy packing up our clothes in preparation for our journey - six o'clock before we arrived at Bourn - ran a tandem to the turnpike - had a narrow escape of our lives.

Tuesday 29th.
Very unpleasant day for the fair - rained as usual - took a walk to J. Osborn's after dinner - very little company in the town - Mr. and Miss Holmes came to dinner - my cousin Betsy joined the party to tea - spent a very pleasant evening.

Wednesday 30th.
Dull morning - never went out the whole day - party came from Aslackby to dine - large party of young ones in the evening - singing and card playing till a late hour - my Father went home.

Thursday 31st.
A delightful morning - some friends called to lunch - went to dine at Mr. J. Osborn's - Mr. Newzam, Miss B. and Mr. Barwis with us - played at cards and dancing in the evening - Mr. and Mrs. Williamson arrived.

Expenses for the month of October:-

	£	s	d
3 oz Lambswool	0	1	6
3 Nails book muslin	0	0	9
2½ Flannel 2/2^d	0	4	9½
2 3/8ths yards Binding	0	0	7
7/8ths worth Trimming	0	2	10
2½ yds Sarsenet ribbon	0	2	1
1 Pair shoes	0	5	0
¾ yds Blk Sarsenet ribbon	0	2	1
¾ yds Black ferret	0	0	3
	0	18	1½

NOVEMBER 1811

Friday 1st.
Mrs. Osborn and family dined with us - Mr. Rudkin returned home - Mr. and Mrs. Bellamy to tea - stopped supper - played at cards - an unpleasant circumstance occurred - the party broke up rather early.

Saturday 2nd.
Weather very uncertain - walked in the market - called upon Mrs. Bellamy and Mrs. Smith - played a game of cards - after dinner went up to my cousin Betsy's to tea and spent the evening.

Sunday 3rd.
A delightful morning - Thomas drove Mrs. Williamson and Miss B. home - was prevented from attending church - called upon Miss Andrews who favoured us with a tune from the grand piano - Mr. and Miss Osborn to tea and supper.

Monday 4th.
Took a walk to John Mawby's shop - purchased a few articles and ordered some bombazeen[1] - called upon Mrs. Shipley - dined with Mrs. Osborn - spent a pleasant day - played at pope[2] in the evening - went to sleep at John Osborn's.

Tuesday 5th.
Cold stormy morning - began to make a box for Catherine - went to Mr. Bellamy's to dine - took a walk in the town in the afternoon - played at pope - spent a pleasant evening - returned to my aunt's to sleep.

Wednesday 6th.
Saw the likeness of Ann Moore and several other curiosities - took a walk up to my cousin Betsy's - finished making the above box - took tea and spent the evening with Mr. Mawby - sounded the bugle horn in the market place and alarmed all the inhabitants who were snug at rest.

Thursday 7th.
Breakfasted with J. Osborn - made several calls in the West Street - dined at home - received company for tea - Miss A. Drew, Miss Lacey, Miss Smith and brothers - played at cards as usual - was highly entertained by singing - upon the whole a very agreeable party.

---

[1] bombazeen – twilled dress material.
[2] pope – a card game for three or more players.

56

NOVEMBER 1811

Friday 8th.
Very unpleasant morning - my Father and Mr. J. Osborn went to Stamford Fair - walked up to town after dinner - purchased a gown for my Mother at Mr. Mawby's - came home to tea - Mr. Corney and Mr. Osborn spent the evening with my cousin John - played at cards.

Saturday 9th.
Fine morning after the rain - arose early to prepare for our journey - took our leave of the family about half past nine - the roads were very bad going through Billingborough - met with Miss Thornton who entreated us to spend the day with her - arrived home at two o'clock.

Sunday 10th.
Very stormy, unpleasant day - could not get to church - had a hare for dinner - felt very little fatigued from my journey yesterday - Mr. Jacques came up in the afternoon but did not stop for tea.

Monday 11th.
Put some of my clothes a little to rights - not much inclined for work today - mended two pairs of stockings - I believe nothing more occurred particular during the remainder of the day - only a bad cold seized my head.

Tuesday 12th.
Very fine morning - washed some small clothes - finished by noon - wrote to Mrs. Scarborough, Boston - sat down to work after dinner - mended two gowns - made a pair of pillow covers.

Wednesday 13th.
Ironed, mangled and laid all the clothes by this morning - Mr. Barnes called on parish affairs - Mr. Nix sent some brandy and gin from Spalding - received some patterns and a note from Mr. Mawby - sat down to play a rubber after supper.

Thursday 14th.
Weather very unpleasant - busy brewing - I was maid in the house - my assistance in the brew house was not required - spinning a little at times - purchased a few articles of Mr. Wilson our merchant - Kirton Statute was very small.

Friday 15th.

Stormy day - the wind remarkably high - churned the butter and helped to make it up - altered our scarlet gowns - my Father went to Spalding Statute - hired a servant - received a bad fall from his horse coming home.

Saturday 16th.

Very busy this morning - got all our work done - dressed by dinner - Mr. Barnet came to pave the stable - Mr. Gleed brought some papers to be signed respecting the game - Mrs. Rudkin called in the afternoon - altered my straw bonnet.

Sunday 17th.

Delightful morning - walked to Gosberton Church - found the roads very clean which is rather unusual at this season of the year - did not go out anywhere after dinner - wrote a letter to my cousin Ann.

Monday 18th.

Began to turn my pelisse[1] - dressed some sheep's tails - man from Pickworth came with goods - sold the rags and a bundle of horse hair - bought some pocket handkerchiefs - Mr. Rudkin and Mrs. Jacques in the evening.

Tuesday 19th.

Sent a parcel to Bourn this morning by Mr. Stubley - made a sheep's tail pie for dinner and did my usual work - finished my pelisse - made it to fit very well - did not think much with the trouble as it looked all the better.

Wednesday 20th.

Very busy all day - up to the elbows in fat - dressed two geese completely and cleaned the giblets - tea time before we finished - played at cards - was obliged to sit up till near two o'clock respecting some work that must be done - wrote a note to Miss Broughton.

---

[1] pelisse – full length cloak.

NOVEMBER 1811

Thursday 21st.
Finished netting a tippet for Miss Broughton - sent it by my Father -
Nanny went to Gosberton with five fat geese and four pairs of giblets -
brought three of them home again - sent them off to Donnington - sold
one - bad success in the goose trade - began spinning a pound of flax –
Mr. Hodson took the locks off the doors - took tea with us - stopped
till eight.

Friday 22nd.
Sharp keen frost this morning - pleasant day for Folkingham Fair - my
Father brought all the beast home again - received a parcel from
Bourn with some patterns of the bombazeen - liked them very well -
sat close to the spinning all day - bad cold.

Saturday 23rd.
Yesterday afternoon, a poor man came with several useful receipts to
dispose of - he had lived with the great cowkeepers in London who at
one time kept nine hundred and ninety nine milking cows - he had
been a prisoner in France for two years and appeared by his discourse
to have seen a great deal of the world - purchased some receipts.

Sunday 24th.
Cold morning - was not at church - my Mother and Father went to
Quadring - roasted a goose for dinner - took a walk in the afternoon -
called upon Mrs. Rudkin - went to Jenny Barratt's - quarrelled with a
dog on the road - the men servants all out.

Monday 25th.
The morning mild and pleasant - up before six - began to spin - sat
very close to the wheel all day - a man very much intoxicated
staggered in while at dinner to call he said out of respect - I believe it
was to the barrel - did not meet with a very pleasant reception so
marched out again.

Tuesday 26th.
The weather remarkably pleasant - as usual arose this morning at five
o'clock to resume the employment before mentioned - sent a parcel to
Bourn by Mr. Rudkin to Spalding - Mr. Spence and Mr. Johnson from
Kirton lunched with us - Mr. Arnall Gleed came to course - the
Widow Hale brought the moping.

NOVEMBER 1811

Wednesday 27th.
Sat down to the wheel as soon as I came downstairs this morning - finished the flax by three o'clock - wound up all the thread and quite completed the web - my Mother began the table linen - our new farmer made his entrance in the evening.

Thursday 28th.
Moonlight morning - but supposing it to be daylight, we all got up and dressed ourselves - was going down in a great bustle when the clock struck three - walked back and after a hearty laugh went to bed again - Mrs. Pickworth called - my right eye very much swelled.

Friday 29th.
Spinning part of the day - my eye very painful - was obliged to wear a shade over it - winding spools in the afternoon - a new sheepdog arrived - half a crown purchase - very lively one - had an application of bread and milk on my eye.

Saturday 30th.
Mild pleasant morning - had a very late breakfast and dinner too - cleaned my wheel ready for Monday - fancied it would almost go alone - blackened all my shoes and boots - eight geese put up to fatten - my eye much the same.

Expenses for the month of November:-

	£	s	d
Book muslin	0	0	10
Purple ribbon	0	1	0
Present	0	1	3
Servant	0	1	0
Ink	0	0	3
Knife	0	1	0
Servant	0	1	0
1 Pocket handkerchief	0	2	4
	0	8	8

DECEMBER 1811

Sunday 1st.
Was not at church - Mr. J. Rudkin came in and stopped till near dinner - Mr. Jacques and Ann walked up in the afternoon - took tea with us - Master Solomon came to accompany them home.

Monday 2nd.
Stormy morning - sat very close to the wheel all day - spun nearly half a pound of flax but was completely tired - a new box pig trough came home in the evening - was much approved of by all but the swinish multitude who appeared very dissatisfied at first sight.

Tuesday 3rd.
Weather as usual - Mrs. Taylor came to wash - I was cook and housemaid - after the business of the morning and dinner was over sat down at the wheel - received an invitation to dine at Mount Pleasant today to meet Mr. and Mrs. Thornton - much work as usual prevented us from going.

Wednesday 4th.
Sharp frosty air proved a very fortunate day for the wash - clothes all dry - spinning most part of the day - helped to mangle a large basket of linen in the afternoon - after tea played at cards - quite against my inclination.

Thursday 5th.
An excessive cold morning - the wind remarkably high and continued freezing very sharp the whole day - the granary was cleaned and washed - kept close to my old companion the wheel till late in the evening.

Friday 6th.
Was very busy all day - finished airing up the clothes - churned and made the butter up before dinner which I considered quite a treat after such a long sitting - my Father went to Gosberton - took tea at Mr. Willerton's.

Saturday 7th.
Cleaned all the rooms - dressed and sat down to spin by eleven - the weaver brought home pieces of napkins - was much delighted with one of the feathered tribe who favoured us with an egg - well satisfied with the week's work - eight weeks' clothes wash and three pounds of flax done - Mr. Daybell, the constable, brought a summons from President Castle.

DECEMBER 1811

Sunday 8th.
Cold stormy day - was prevented from attending church - Mr. and Mrs. Rudkin came to tea with Mr. John - did not stop to supper - saw a young gentleman going to a party in a new fashioned dress - Mr. J. sent for the kitts[1].

Monday 9th.
Arose early this morning - spinning from five to eleven then had the dairy and breakfast to attend to - mended my morning gowns - had three spools to wind - Mrs. Pickworth sent to enquire after the family.

Tuesday 10th.
Very uncomfortable morning - the wind was remarkably high - began to spin at five o'clock - spun half a pound of flax which I accomplished by eight in the evening - very much tired.

Wednesday 11th.
Fine morning but very frosty - my Father went to Boston Mart on some unpleasant business respecting the roads - Mr. Pickworth called as he returned home - winding spools in the evening..

Thursday 12th.
Foggy morning - took a walk to the town and a very unpleasant one it proved - lunched at Mr. Willerton's - settled accounts - bought some towelling - ordered some paint - sold two geese - wound eight spools and quite completed the web.

Friday 13th.
Mild morning - after breakfast began to clean the kitchen fireplace which served me the whole day - put an end to all the whitewash and clothed it in black - painted the brickwork ready for the white.

Saturday 14th.
Cold morning - the wind high - just as I had accomplished the above painting was very much surprised by a visitor - Mr. J. Osborn - received a note with a song from my cousin Ann and a parcel which contained our winter dresses - liked them very well - dressed a couple of fowls - played at cards.

---

[1] kitts – kittens.

DECEMBER 1811

Sunday 15th.
Very indifferent account of church today which well too often appears in the latter part of this book - wrote a note to Miss A. Osborn - my cousin returned home after dinner - remitted the account to Mr. Mawby for the above parcel - Mr. Jacques and son to supper - the latter with Drakard's nonsensical paper.

Monday 16th.
Very cold and remarkably stormy particularly towards evening - cleaned the little room and B. chamber - turned the bed in my Mother's room which made a great alteration - began to make Nanny's gowns.

Tuesday 17th.
A pleasant morning - my Father went to Spalding Market - bought an almanac and a quire of writing paper - a family out of Leicestershire rather of a darkish appearance called in the morning - mended the lantern - finished Nanny's gowns and began to dissect the ruby stuffs.

Wednesday 18th.
One of the fat pigs killed this morning - Mr. Wheat called for an order but received none - sat at work at gowns all day - finished the skirts and sleeves - Mr. Arnall Gleed came a coursing - marked some coarse linen - sent to the town for some groceries.

Thursday 19th.
A fine morning - rendered the ears - sorted the meat ready for the pies - finished all by dinner - the pig weighed twenty three stones - worked at the gowns while tea - picked some raisins - played two rubbers till supper was ready and lost them both.

Friday 20th.
Busy day - made pork pies, mince pies and sausages - churning and baked twice - everything appeared to go on rather awkward - it was late before we had finished - had a fresh supply of oil cakes[1] in - played two rubbers - lost them both as usual.

---

[1] oil cakes – cattle food made from compressed linseed.

DECEMBER 1811

Saturday 21st.
Arose this morning at six o'clock - had the kitchen and dairy washed before breakfast - cleaned the chambers - made a large pork pie for dinner - my Father went to Donnington Market - mended me half boots.

Sunday 22nd.
Sharp frosty day - was not at church - cut the paper for my new journal and drawed the lines for the first month - eight o'clock in the evening read the thirtieth chapter of Isaiah - Mr. Jacques came.

Monday 23rd.
Mild pleasant morning - arose at five - killed eight geese - stripped four before breakfast - drawed half a dozen of them - giblets cleaned and all done by five - ready to attend the gentlemen Mr. Green and Mr. Ranby who came to tea - passed the evening very pleasantly.

Tuesday 24th.
Very busy this morning - packing up the geese and giblets - sent them in - baked bread and Yule cakes - cleaned the parlour - two gipsies called with violins and tambourines - played several tunes in a very masterly style - delightful to hear - played at cards.

Wednesday 25th.
Christmas day - sharp frost - did not go to church - Mr. Cooper brought his bill - had two large plumb puddings and two geese for dinner - received a parcel of prints from Mr. Mawby and a letter from my cousin Ann - Mr. Jacques as usual - reading and writing in the evening.

Thursday 26th.
Cold morning - finished making our gowns - a number of trade's people called for their Christmas boxes - lined the purple gown's sleeves - three more musicians favoured us with a call but very inferior to the above party - played at cards as usual.

Friday 27th.
Sharp frosty morning - dressed and intended walking to Mr. Pickworth's to dine but was prevented by the fall of snow - very much disappointed - in addition to the musical list, we were visited by a party of Morris dancers - very smartly dressed - each acting their part as they entered - danced a reel, sung a duet and the whole was performed remarkably well.

DECEMBER 1811

Saturday 28th.

The weather very unpleasant - snowed fast - did not rise this morning till a late hour - got all our work done and dressed before dinner which is rather unusual for a Saturday - was obliged to sit to work by the kitchen fire on account of the smoke - covered my journal for the ensuing year - played at cards in the evening.

Sunday 29th.

Was not at church - very cold day - snowed most part of the afternoon - Mr. Jacques called - brought a letter for us to peruse that he received from America which contained great intelligence from that country - wrote a letter in the evening.

Monday 30th.

Piercing cold morning - finished making my old stuff gown close - nothing particular happened during the day - made up a parcel to send to Bourn but could not find a friend to convey it to Spalding - played at cards as usual.

Tuesday 31st.

Very little alteration in respect of the weather - made a pair of mitts and some cap borders - mended coats - played at cards in the evening - very unlucky as usual to the end of the year - but being unfortunate at cards I consider a mere trifle.

Expenses for the month of December:-

	£	s	d
3 Nails muslin	0	0	4½
6 yds ¾ Maroon stuff 2/-	0	13	6
2 yds ¼ Ribbon 8^d	0	1	6
Silk and cotton	0	0	3
Writing paper	0	1	0
Pink dye	0	0	6
1 yd Black galloon [1]	0	0	2
Wire buttons	0	0	4
Card paper	0	0	3
	0	17	10½

---

[1] galloon – a narrow, close-woven braid.

The Total of Expenses for the whole of the year:-

	£	s	d
January...................	0	14	10
February.................	0	7	8½
March....................	0	12	2½
April.....................	0	5	11½
May......................	2	11	1
June......................	1	5	7¼
July......................	1	13	7½
August...................	1	2	8½
September...............	0	2	6
October..................	0	18	1½
November................	0	8	8
December................	0	17	10½
	11	**0**	**10¾**
Paid out of my own purse	**6**	**10**	**10**

Songs and Poetry

Recorded on the reverse pages of the diary.

Love and Glory

Young Henry was as brave a youth
As ever graced a martial story,
And Jane was fair as lovely truth
She sighed for love and he for glory.

With her his faith he meant to flight
And told her many a gallant story,
Till war - honest joys to blight
Called him away from love to glory.

Brave Henry smote the foe with pride
Jane followed - fought - oh hapless story,
In man's attire by Henry's side
She died for love and he for glory.

May I Perish if Ever I Plant In That Bosom A Thorn.

From the white blossom'd sloe my dear Chloe requested
A sprig her fair breast to adorn,
No by heavens I exclaimed may I perish if ever
I plant in that bosom a thorn.

When I showed her a ring and implored her to marry,
She blushed like the dawning of morn,
Yes I'll consent she replied if you promise
That no jealous rival shall laugh me to scorn,
No by heavens I explained may I perish if ever
I plant in that bosom a thorn.

Since I've gained her consent I'll endeavour to please her
And live to protect her from harm,
No by heavens I exclaimed may I perish if ever
I plant in that bosom a thorn.

The Smile and the Tear.

Said a smile to a tear on the cheek of my dear,
Which beamed like the sun in spring weather,
In sooth lovely tear it strange doth appear,
That we should be both here together.

I come from the heart a soft balm to impart,
To yonder our daughter of grief,
And I said the smile that heart to beguile,
Since you gave the poor mourner relief.

Oh there, said the tear, sweet smile it is clear,
We are twins and soft pity our mistress,
And how lovely that face which together we grace,
For the woe and the bliss of another.

Just Like Love.

First/

    Just like love is yonder rose,
    Heavenly fragrance round it throws,
    Tears its dewy leaves disclose,
    And in the midst of briers it blows.
    Just like love, just like love, just like love.

Second/

    Call'd to bloom upon the breast,
    Since rough thorns the stem invest,
    They must be gathered with the rest,
    And with it the heart be prest.
    Just like love, just like love, just like love.

Third/

    And when rude hands the twin buds sever,
    They die and they shed blossoms never,
    Yet the thorn be sharp as ever,
    Yet the thorn be sharp as ever.
    Just like love, just like love, just like love.

My Beautiful Maid.

When absent from her whom my soul holds most dear,
What medley of passions invade,
In this bosom what anguish what hope and what fear,
I endure for my beautiful maid.

In vain I seek pleasure to lighten my grief,
Or quit the gay throng for the shade,
Nor retirement nor solitude yield me relief,
When away from my beautiful maid.

The Maid of Lodi.

I sing the Maid of Lodi
Who sweetly sang to me,
Whose brows were never clouded
Nor e'er distort with glee.
She values not the wealthy
Unless they're great and good,
For she is strong and healthy
And by labour comes her food.

And when her day's work's over
Around a cheerful fire,
She sings or rests contented
What more can man desire.
Let those who squander millions
Review her happy lot,
They'll find their proud pavilions
Far inferior to a cot.

Between the Po and Poma
Some villain seized my coach,
And dragged me to a cavern
Most dreadful to approach.
By which the Maid of Lodi
Came a strolling from the fair,
She paused to hear my wailings
And saw me tear my hair.

Then to her market basket
She tied her pony's reins,
I thus by female courage
Was dragged to life again.
She led me to her dwelling
She cheered my heart with wine,
And then she decked her table
At which the gods might dine.

Among the smile Madonna
Her features you may find,
But not the famed Carrigio
Could ever paint her mind.
Then sing the Maid of Lodi
Who sweetly sang to me,
And when this maid is married
Still happier may she be.

Lodi: A town In Italy. In 1804 Lord Byron declared that "The Maid of Lodi" was his favourite song.

Oh No, My Love, No.

While I hang on your bosom distracted to lose you,
High swells my sad heart and fast my tears flow,
Yet think not of coldness, they fail to accuse you,
Did I ever upbraid you? Oh no, my love, no.

I own it would please me at home would you tarry,
Nor e'er feel a wish from your Fanny to go,
But if it gives pleasure to you my dear Harry,
Shall I blame your departure? Oh no, my love, no.

Now do not dear Hal while abroad you are straying,
That heart which is mine on a rival bestow,
Nay, banish that frown such displeasure betraying,
Do you think I suspect you? Oh no, my love, no.

I believe you're too kind for one moment to grieve me,
Or plant in a heart which adores you such woe,
Yet should you dishonour my truth and deceive me,
Should I e'er cease to love you? Oh no, my love, no.

The Rosy Dawn.

When the rosy morn appearing
Paints with gold the verdant lawn,
Bees on banks of thyme disporting
Sip the sweets and hail the dawn.

Warbling birds the day proclaiming
Carol sweet the lively strain,
They forsake their leafy dwellings
To scour the golden grain.

See content the humble gleaner
Take the scattered ears that fall,
Nature all her children viewing
Kindly bounteous cares for all.

The Trumpet Sounds.

He was famed for deeds of arms,
She a maid of envy'd charms,
Now to him her love imparts,
One pure flame pervades both hearts.
Honour calls him to the field,
Love to conquest now must yield,
Sweet maid he cried again I'll come to thee,
When the glad trumpet sounds a victory.

Battle now with fury glows,
Hostile blood in torrents flows,
His duty tells him to depart,
She pressed her hero to her heart,
Sweet maid he cried again I'll come to thee,
When the glad trumpet sounds a victory.

He with love and conquest burns,
Both subdued his mind by turns,
Death the soldier now enthrals,
With the wounds the hero falls,
She disdaining war's alarms,
Blushed and caught him in her arms,
Oh death he cries thou'rt welcome now to me,
For hark the trumpet sounds a victory.

Oh, Love Me Evermore.

In either eye a lingering tear
His love and duty well to prove,
Jack left his wife and children dear
Impell'd by honour and by love,
And as he loitered enrapt in care
A sapling in his hand he bore,
Curiously carved in letters fair
Love me, oh love me evermore.

At leisure to behold his worth
Tokens and rings and broken gold,
He plunged the sapling firm in earth
And o'er and o'er his treasure told,
The letters spelt his kindness trac'd,
And all affections precious store,
Each with the favourite motto grac'd
Love me, oh love me evermore.

While on this anxious task employ'd
Tender remembrance all his care,
His ears were suddenly annoyed
The boatswain's whistle cleaves the air,
His duty call, his nerves are braced
He rushes to the crowded shore,
Leaving the sapling in his haste
That bids him love for evermore.

The magic branch thus unreclaimed
Far off at sea no comfort near,
His thoughtless haste he loudly blamed
With many a sigh and many a tear,
Yet why act this unmanly part,
The words the precious relic bore,
Are they not marked upon my heart
Love me, oh love me evermore.

Escaped from treacherous waves and winds
That three years he had felt at sea,
A wond'rous miracle he finds
The sapling is become a tree,

A goodly head that graceful rears
Enlarged the trunk enlarged the core,
And on the rind enlarged appears
Love me, oh love me evermore.

While gazing on the spell-like charms
On this most wonderful of trees,
His Nancy rushes to his arms
His children cling about his knees,
Increased in love, increased in size
Taught from the mother's tender care,
Each little urchin lisping cries
Love me, oh love me for evermore.

Amazement seized the admiring crowd,
My children cried a village seer,
I have signs though mute declare aloud
The hand of providence is here,
Whose hidden yet whose sure decrees,
For those its succour who implore,
Can still the tempest level seas
And crown true love for evermore.

Begone Dull Care.

Begone dull care
I prithee begone from me,
Begone dull care
You and I shall never agree,
Long time hast thou been tarrying here
And fain then would'st me kill,
But in faith dull care
Thou never shall have thy will.

Too much care
Will make a young man grey,
And too much care
Will turn an old man to clay,
My wife shall dance and I will sing
So merrily pass the day,
For I hold it one of wisest things
To drive dull care away.

The Song Of Young Lobster.

Young Lobster said to his ugly wife
I'm off till tomorrow to fish my life,
Says Mistress Lobster I'm sure you a'nt
You brute you're going to galivant.
To Galivant etc...........

What Mistress Lobster said was right
Gay Mr. Lobster staid out all night,
He ne'er went afishing 'tis known very well
But where he went I shall not tell.
I shall not tell.............

Next morning Mr. Lobster knew
He'd caught no fish so he bought a few,
Says he my wife won't smoke the plot
And she will bite tho' the fish did not.
The fish did not............

Young Lobster to his spouse drew near
Says she what sport have you had my dear,
The river says he is full of water rats
So I've only caught you a dozen sprats.

A dozen sprats, base man says she
What! Catch in the river the fish of the sea,
You can draw a long line Mr. L. I know
But 'tis clear you can draw a much longer bow.

Let all men who are frail in flesh
Observe salt water is not fresh,
For wives then husbands well condemn
Who think with sprats to gudgeon them.

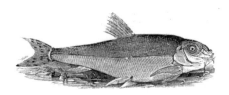

GUDGEON.

74

Tol, Lol De Rol.

I'ze a poor country lad as you see by my dress,
That I'ze Yorkshire may hap you may pretty well guess,
My name's Zekeil Homespun you all know me now,
It is not the first time I have here made my bow.
Tol, lol de rol, etc.

To London I com'd upon business d'ye see,
But contrived to make pleasure and business agree,
For when I gets back, wi' our chaps on the green,
They'll be sure to be axing me what I ha' seen.
Tol, lol de rol, etc.

Now having in town but a short time to stay,
Thinks I, while the sun shines, I'd better make hay,
So I ax'd what the play were, they told me by gum,
Twas a very fine tragedy call'd Tommy Thumb.
Tol, lol de rol, etc.

In Yorkshire, I'd oft heard our knowing ones say,
That a very good moral was learned from a play,
And that tragedy boasted of language so fine,
So I thought that as how it might help me wi' mine.
Tol, lol de rol, etc.

Well, the curtain drew up and the first to appear,
Were two gentlemen drest to be sure mortal queer,
Says one, "To the king this petition I'll shew,"
Then the other to him answered, "Do, doodle, do."
Tol, lol de rol, etc.

In the next scene were king and queen on the throne,
To whom the petition was presently shewn,
But King Arthur from Doodle indignantly shrunk,
For says he, "Tis our pleasure this day to get drunk."
Tol, lol de rol, etc.

So thinks I to myself an' that's what you're about,
There's no business for me sure see the play out,
To my own native parts I quickly get down,
I can learn to get drunk there as well as in town.
Tol, lol de rol, etc.

So I'ze ta'en me a place at the George and Blue Boar,
Where the coach will set off in the morning at four,
And as I must be up long afore it is light,
I hope you'll not keep me here too late t'night.

Tol, lol de rol, etc. etc.

The favourite tune of the Local Militias when at Boston.

What Is Glory?

What is glory, what is fame,
That a shadow, this a name,
Restless mortals to deceive,
Are they renown, can they be great,
Who hurt their fellow creatures' fate,
That mothers, children, wives may grieve,
Who smiling honour to proclaim,
What is glory what is fame?

Hark the glad mandate strikes the listening ear,
The truest glory to the bosom dear,
Is when the souls starts soft compassions tear.

What are riches, pomp and power,
Gewgaws that endure their hour,
Wretched mortals to allure,
Can greatness reach the idly vain,
Indulging in the princely fain,
Deaf to the miseries of the poor,
Also smiling reason to proclaim,
What is glory, what is fame?

Hark the sweet mandate strikes the listening ear,
The truest glory to the bosom dear
Is when the souls starts soft compassions tear.

Fair Ellen.

Fair Ellen like a lily grew,
Was beauty's fav'rite flower,
Till falsehood chang'd her lovely hue,
She wither'd in an hour.

Antonio, in her virgin breast,
First sow'd a tender sigh,
His wish obtain'd, the lover blest,
Then left the maid to die.

Far, far from me my lover flies,
A faithless lover he,
In vain my tears, in vain my sighs,
No longer true to me,
He seeks, he seeks another.

Lie still my heart no longer grieve,
Nor pangs to him betray,
Who brought you these sad sighs to heave,
And laughing went away,
To seek, to seek another.

A Good Name.

Ere around the huge oak that o'ershadows the mill,
The fond ivy had dared to entwine,
Ere the church was a ruin that nods on the hill,
Or a rook built its nest on the pine.

Could I travel back the time to a far distant date,
Since my forefathers toiled in the field,
And the farm I now hold on your honour's estate,
Is the same which my grandfather tilled.

He dying bequeathed to his son a good name,
Which unsully'd descended to me,
For my child I've preserved it unblemished with shame,
And it still from a spot shall be free.

Fairest Of The Fair.

Oh, Nanny wilt thou fly with me
Nor sigh to leave the charming town,
Can silent glens have charms for thee
The lowly cot and russet gown,
No longer drest in silken sheen
No longer drest in jewels rare,
Say can'st thou quit the busy scene
Where thou were fairest of the fair.

Oh Nanny when thou'rt far away
Will thou not cast a wish behind,
Say can'st thou face the flaky snow
Nor shrink before the warping wind,
Or can that soft and gentlest mien
Severest hardships learn to bear,
Nor sad regret each courtly scene
More than wert fairest of the fair.

Oh Nanny can'st thou love so true
Thro' perils keen with me to go,
Or when thy swain mishap shall rue
To share with him the pangs of woe,
And when invading pain befall
Wilt thou assume the nurse's care,
Nor wishful those gay scenes recall
Where thou were fairest of the fair.

And when at last thy love shall die
Wilt thou receive his parting breath,
Wilt thou repress each struggling sigh
And cheer with smiles the bed of death,
And wilt thou o'er his much loved clay
Strew flowers and drop the tender tear,
Now then regret those scenes so gay
Where thou wert fairest of the fair.

Clerical Comfort.

To the corpse of the vicar the curate was eyeing,
Oh grieve not said his spouse for the dying.
Tis good, the advice, cried the Curate, you're giving
For I muse on the dead, but I think of the living.

Hearty Good Fellow.

With my pipe in my hand and my jug in the other
I drink to my neighbours and friends,
All my care in a whiff of tobacco I smother
For life I know shortly must end.

For whilst Ceres most kindly refills my brown jug
With good liquor I'll make myself mellow,
In an old wicker chair I'll seat myself snug
Like a jolly and true hearted fellow.

I'll ne'er trouble my head with the cares of the nation
I've enough of my own for to mind,
For the cares of this life are but grief and vexation
To death we must all be consigned.

Then I'll laugh, drink and smoak and leave nothing to pay
But drop like a pear that is mellow,
And when cold in my coffin I'll leave them to say
He's gone. What a hearty good fellow.

PROVERBS and SAYINGS.
Recorded on the reverse pages of the diary.

When you wish to be comfortable give a neat dinner to a small party. When you wish to be uncomfortable give a great dinner to a large party.

Strictly speaking no man is independent. The shoemaker, if he pleases, may compel the nobleman to walk in his stockings.

What maintains one vice would maintain two children.

Politicians are like a flock of sheep. If the great men jump over a straw, the whole flock will do the same without knowing why or wherefore.

Where you find the most obstinacy there you will find the most ignorance.

I never see a child but I think of the miseries it has to go through.

The stomach tires of everything but bread and water.

The shortest way to the churchyard is to pass through the dram shop.

Meat that is put upon the table ill-dressed is half wasted.

A pack of hounds is more easily managed than a pack of idle servants.

She is not a good housewife who is always buying pennyworths.

A mild tempered woman is the balsam that heals all human sorrows but a perverse woman is a perpetual blister.

An obedient wife commands her husband.

A woman who is continually contradicting her husband in trifling matters will soon teach him to despise her.

Marrying a man you dislike in hope of loving him afterwards is like going to sea in a storm in the hope of fair weather.

If you have a numerous family of young children, your wife must learn the art of staying at home.

Work hard when you are young that you may play when you are old.

Industry is more valuable in a woman than accomplishments.

There are parsons who would rather say a parish grace than preach a parish sermon.

In most affairs take the opinion of a friend, but take your own at last when duly formed.

A woman should not be denied a reasonable share of amusement though she never appears more amiable than when employed in the duties of her family.

If you marry a violent and imperious woman you may consider yourself as sent to the house of correction for life.

An oyster shows more sense than a prating woman as it never opens its mouth but when the tide is coming in.

Many women have got good husbands by being occasionally seen with aprons on.

It shows a great want of judgment in a married woman to be always struggling for the last word.

The five alls are represented by a king who says "I rule all", a soldier who says "I fight for all", a parson who says "I pray for all", a lawyer who says "I plead for all" and a farmer who says "I pay for all".

Quotations From The Stamford Mercury.

These are also recorded on the reverse of the diary.

The following is understood to be the origin of the old adage - If it rains on St. Swithin's day etc., etc.

For the year 865, St. Swithin Bishop of Winchester dying, was canonized by the then Pope. He was singular in his desire to be buried in the open churchyard and not in the chancel of the Minster as was usual with the then bishops, which request was complied with; but the monks on his being canonized, taking it into their heads that it was disgraceful for the saint to be in the open churchyard, resolved to move his body into the choir which was to have been done in solemn procession on the 15th July. It however rained so violently on that day and forty days succeeding as had hardly ever been known which made them set aside their design, as contrary to the will of heaven, and instead of removing the body they erected a chapel over his grave.
Stamford Mercury August 16th. 1811.

1811. As taken from the Old Stamford Paper August 16th. - stated to be a fact.

There is a remarkable oak tree at Hendre, near Denbigh in the farmyard of the Rev'd W. Chambers, its base is 33 feet in circumference; 15 feet from the ground it is 30 feet in circumference. Only one solitary branch remains in verdure in this venerable trunk, and strange and ignoble reverse, that Monarch of the woods forms a pigsty, capable of accommodating near a score of the swinish multitude.

Last week a gooseberry was plucked in the garden of W. Dickenson, at Rothersoke, near Egremont which measured four and a half inches in circumference and weighed three ounces and one penny-weight.

Index of Persons

Pickworth Mr., 11, 13, 14, 21, , 23, 25, 32, 33, 35, 38, 52, 62, 64

Pickworth Mrs., 11, 12, 14, 20, 21, 22, 26, 29, 30, 31, 34, 36, 37, 48, 49, 50, 60, 62

Pyecroft Junior Mr., 20

Raddish Mr., 41

Ranby Mr., 21, 64

Robert, 4, 15, 31

Robinson Mrs., 22

Root Mr., 23

Roper Miss, 32, 34, 47

Rudkin J. Mr. and Mrs., 31

Rudkin John, 1, 42, 48

Rudkin John Mr., 3, 9, 18, 27, 47, 49, 62

Rudkin Mr. and Mrs., 1, 11, 18, 47, 49, 51, 62

Rudkin Mr., 11, 12, 19, 50, 56, 58, 59

Rudkin Mrs., 8, 12, 13, 20, 25, 30, 32, 35, 38, 41, 43, 46, 50, 53, 58, 59

Scarborough Mrs., 51, 57

Seward Mrs., 21, 54

Shipley Master, 36

Shipley Mr., 27

Shipley Mrs., 3, 56

Sidney James Mr., 47

Simms Miss, 24, 26, 27, 29, 36, 48

Slater Jenny, 14

Smedley Mrs., 14

Smith Mr., 4

Smith Creasey Mrs., 21

Smith Miss, 3, 4, 20, 56

Smith Mrs., 21, 56

Smith Robert Mr., 53

Solomon Master, 61

Spence Mr., 59

Stevenson, 9, 15, 20, 33

Stott Mr., 21

Stredder Mr., 44

Stubbleday Mr., 23

Stubley Mr., 54, 58

Syson Mr., 18, 25, 40, 44, 54

Syson Mrs., 25, 36, 43, 44, 54

Taylor Mary, 25

Taylor Miss, 8

Taylor Mrs., 61

Thompson, 33

Thompson Mrs., 21

Thornton Miss, 14, 36, 57

Thornton Mr. and Mrs., 61

Thornton Mr., 37

Tomlingson Mr., 23

Ward Bet, 44

Ward Mr., 37, 46

Weatherhog Miss, 41, 43

Westmorland Mrs., 37

Wheat Mr., 1, 6, 32, 40, 63

Wheat Mrs., 18, 49

Willerton John, 43

Willerton Mr., 6, 7, 8, 25, 30, 49, 53, 61, 62

Willerton Mrs., 38, 41

Williamson Miss, 35, 41

Williamson Mr., 41

Williamson Mr. and Mrs., 35, 55

Williamson Mrs., 41, 56

Wilson Mr., 46, 57

Wingad, 32

Winger, 40

Yerburgh Mr., 53

Index of Places

Index of First Lines - Songs and Poetry